ENDORSEMENTS

This timely book is a must-read for every believer, especially now. Pastor Andre Butler points out that a believer doesn't have to be a victim simply because of tough economic times. He shows you in the Word that when believers are obedient, God separates them from the disturbances of the world. Read this book today, and you will find out how.

—Bishop Keith A. Butler, founder/pastor of
Word of Faith International Christian Center,
Southfield, Michigan (www.woficc.com)

This book is very encouraging for those who have been faithfully serving God and have kept His commandments, as they can expect to experience firsthand the promises of His covenant. Every born-again believer should read and take heed of this wise man of God as he alerts the body of Christ to be sober, vigilant, and prepared for what's to come in this crucial time in history.

—George L. Davis, senior pastor of
Faith Christian Center, Jacksonville, Florida

I thank God for Pastor Andre Butler being bold enough to write a book saying what God says and teaching us how we can make it through this current economic climate. I agree with Pastor Butler: Not in my house! We will not participate in the recession!

—Bishop Gregory M. Davis Sr.,
River of Life Church, host of Rejoice in the Word
(www.gregdavisministries.com)

Andre Butler has written *Not in My House,* taken the bull by the horns and addressed the fundamental financial issue facing Christians today: Will we stand, or will we fall? He integrates sound biblical principles with practical strategies that can readily turn anyone's recessionary fears into financial protection and growth. A must-read for everyone.

—Catherine Eagan, CEO of The Wealthy Women Club, financial expert, author, and speaker (www.catherineeagan.com)

Not in My House is a work of superb clarity filled with solid biblical answers to the prevailing economic crisis facing us today. Butler offers a new paradigm and plan for anyone wanting to push past circumstances and prosper in spite of them. It is an extraordinary work that must be read by those interested in recession-proofing their future!

—Dr. James Pierce, author of *Success Secrets of Excellence* and senior pastor of Life Changers Christian Center, Lansing, Michigan (www.lifechangerscc.org)

Pastor Andre Butler is intense about God's Word and His Spirit. God has given him insights on how to prosper in times of recession. I encourage you to devour very page in his book. As you apply it in your life, you will experience the blessings of God. See you at the top!

—Dr. Nasir K Siddiki, author of *Kingdom Principles of Financial Increase* (www.wisdomministries.org)

I believe in Pastor Andre's latest book, *Not in My House.* He teaches that we don't have to cooperate with today's recession. We can still have an utmost life in the midst of "almost" times. I wholeheartedly believe in that.

—Dr. Tim Storey, speaker, life coach, and author of *Utmost Living: Creating and Savoring Your Best Life Now* (www.timstoreyonline.com)

NOT IN MY HOUSE!

NOT IN MY HOUSE!

TAKE THE 28-DAY CHALLENGE TO RECESSION-PROOF YOUR FUTURE

ANDRE BUTLER

Not in My House by Andre Butler

Published by HigherLife Press
2342 Westminster Terrace
Oviedo, Florida 32765
(407) 563-4806
www.ahigherlife.com

Unless otherwise noted, Scriptures are taken from the King James Version of the Bible.

Scriptures marked AMP are taken from the Amplified® Bible, Copyright © 1954, 1958, 1962, 1964, 1965, 1987 by The Lockman Foundation. Used by permission. (www.lockman.org)

ISBN: 978-0-9793227-3-0

09 10 11 12 13 – 8 7 6 5 4 3 2 1

Printed in the United States of America

DEDICATION

*To my wonderful wife, Tiffany (there is no spot in thee!),
and my three little blessings, Alexis, Angela, and April.*

TABLE OF CONTENTS

Week 1: No Recession Here

Week 2: God's Riches in Glory

Week 3: Switching Banks

Week 4: No More Debt

FOREWORD

I'VE KNOWN PASTOR ANDRE BUTLER FOR MANY YEARS, AND I'VE seen him grow into a powerful preacher of the Word of God and anointed to teach on prosperity. He is a great example of how God will bless you if you really live for Him.

He has written an "on-time" word for this season of financial instability that has hit Wall Street. Many people today are fearfully concerned about the housing market, the banking system, fluctuating gasoline prices, and the economy overall—even Christians. God's will for our lives isn't that we be afraid of lack. He's a God of supernatural increase. He's a God of abundance, and His plan for us is that we have more than enough.

In *Not in My House,* Pastor Andre shows you, through the Scriptures, how to recession-proof your life now and in the future. This book will build up your faith and show you how to flourish and be a beacon of hope for others. Just like Joseph flourished during the famine in Egypt (see Gen. 41:46-57), Christians also can prosper in a declining economy.

Pastor Andre reminds us that God will take care of us if we seek Him first. He rightly says that many people are hurting because they've invested in the wrong system. After reading this book, you will be inspired to "switch banks" and invest in the Bank of Heaven—and there's never a recession in heaven!

As you take the twenty-eight-day challenge, you will be encouraged and blessed yourself—and then you will be in a stronger position to be a blessing to others.

—Kate McVeigh, author,
The Blessing of Favor
(www.katemcveigh.org)

ACKNOWLEDGEMENTS

I WOULD LIKE TO GIVE HONOR TO MY LORD AND SAVIOR, JESUS Christ, who has saved me and given me the honor of helping Him save the world. Also to my parents and sisters, Bishop Keith Butler, Pastor Deborah Butler, Pastor MiChelle Butler, and Minister Kristina Butler. Without all of you, I would not be who I am. I also would like to acknowledge Rev. Kenneth E. Hagin, Rev. Kenneth W. Hagin, Kenneth and Gloria Copeland, and the many other outstanding men and women of God who have taught me the Word of faith. I am forever grateful!

INTRODUCTION

WHEN I SAT DOWN TO WRITE THIS BOOK, I KNEW I WANTED to make it very practical and encouraging. Nobody wants to read a dry financial treatise, and you're not going to find that here. What you will find is both inspiration and motivation—so that you can make the same declaration I made, which you'll read about on day 1. Throughout the book, you'll find practical and proven tools to help you do that.

Here's how the challenge works:

Step 1: Buy the book.

Step 2: Keep up with the readings every day.

Step 3: Meet weekly with a small group to discuss the questions at the end of each week.

Step 4: Complete the action step for the week.

Step 5: Buy a book for a friend and encourage him or her to take the twenty-eight-day challenge, too.

The book is divided into four weeks. Each week has five days of readings, which you'll do on your own, then some guidelines and suggested questions for you to cover at a small-group meeting. Small groups are helpful when you're undertaking a challenge like this one. The other people in the group will provide the encouragement, motivation and pats on the back (and sometimes kicks in the pants) that you'll need to successfully reach the last day of the challenge. The seventh day each week is a day of rest; I've given you a short thought that you can meditate on throughout that day.

As you study each reading, remember that God's purpose behind the Scripture passages we'll read is not solely financial, even though those verses talk about finances. Clearly, throughout the Bible, God was accomplishing greater things than solely taking care of His people's bottom line, as is true today as well. God is interested most of all in winning the world to Himself and in His people doing their part to make disciples for Him.

We'll talk a lot about financial prosperity, but that is the lowest type of prosperity. Unfortunately, it is the one part of prosperity that God's people lack and have been deceived about. Yet, God wants us to have it so we experience His blessings and, even more importantly, so His purposes in the earth—winning the lost—can be fully accomplished.

Are you ready to take the challenge? Let's begin.

Week 1

NO RECESSION HERE

Day 1

JUST SAY NO

I've made a decision: I'm not going to participate in the recession. You know, the recession that's all over the news? The one that every newspaper reporter and TV correspondent is talking about? The one that half the world is panicked about?

I simply decided I'm not going to join them. If they want to wallow in recession, that's up to them—but I'm not going to participate. Recession? I've decided to just say no.

Instead, I'm spending my time doing three things. First, I'm making my house recession-proof. Second, I'm preparing for God to bring increase in every area of my life. And third, I'm writing this book to tell you why you don't have to participate in the recession, either—and to show you exactly how to recession-proof your own house.

Please understand, I'm not denying that the world is in bad shape economically. It's happening all around us. The world is going through a deep financial crisis because the United States is going through a financial crisis. There's a mortgage crisis and a credit crisis. The stock market is on a roller coaster. People are struggling, losing their jobs, their retirements, their savings, and their homes. They're worried about their IRAs, their 401Ks and their HSAs. It's no wonder that most people are afraid.

We, however, are not "most people." God called us a peculiar people, a people set apart. While the world goes through a recession, as followers of Jesus, we don't have to. While the world caves in to fear, we know that "God hath not given us the spirit of fear; but of power, and of love, and of a sound mind" (2 Tim. 1:7). Financial ruin and the fear that accompanies it can happen all around us, but they don't have to happen to us. Instead, we can look and see that the wealth of the sinner is getting ready to come into the hands of the just. This is not only for our benefit; it is part of God's plan to expand His kingdom to the ends of the earth. Someone has to finance it, and who better to do that than God's people?

You can be God's instrument to minister to a world drowning in recession. In fact, God wants you to do that.

What the world is going through is not so much a recession as it is a restructuring. God is getting ready to do something for us and through us—and we must be prepared. The time is here. Let me repeat that: The time is here.

The world may be participating in a recession, but you don't have to. You can refuse to participate. You can choose to recession-proof your house. You can keep your job. You can keep your home. You can keep your car and keep it filled with gas. You can keep money in your savings account and have funds stored up to help those around you.

In fact, while the world is losing money, you can be in the middle of the very same circumstances, but instead, you can be increased. You can be in a position to help your family and all those around you. You can be God's instrument to minister to a world drowning in recession. In fact, God wants you to do that.

I pray I'm filling you with hope because that's exactly what I want to do. God promises there is "hope for your future" (Jer. 31:17 AMP). You have a choice. You can make the same decision I did, not to participate in the recession. Like me, you can just say no.

Let me give you a testimony of what happened when my wife and I made the decision not to participate in the recession. In the next few weeks, we saw a manifestation of tens of thousands of dollars of harvest. Suddenly, things we had been believing God to provide for years started to happen. Phone calls came, information arrived, and God provided for us in miraculous ways. My wife and I have been believing God to eliminate our car notes, for example. I received a phone call from a Christian businessman in our church who said God told him to bless us in this arena. He later wrote us a check for tens of thousands of dollars to eliminate our car notes!

Let me be clear that the blessings we began to see were not just for us, but also for us to bless others. While those in the world around us are throwing their hands in the air and worrying about losing what they possess, we as believers are seeing God increase us, reduce our debt, and position us for even more increase in the days to come so we can bless others.

Isn't that what you want, too? You don't want your increase to be on "pause." You don't want to have to wait until the recession is over before you start believing God, before you start seeing debts canceled, before you start seeing the dreams in your heart fully manifest. You don't want to wait until the world gets its act together before you receive what God promised you—and before you can share those blessings with a hurting world.

I've got good news for you: You don't have to wait. If you are following Jesus as your Lord and Savior, the ups and downs of the economy should have no real impact on your financial life. You are *in* the world, but not *of* the world.

"Oh, Brother Andre," you might say, "you don't know the financial situation I'm in. You don't know the hole I've dug for myself. And even if I wanted to believe you, where is that in the Bible? Where did God say we don't have to participate in a recession? Is that scriptural?"

Yes, it is. There's that minor incident in the Old Testament of 2 million children of Israel refusing to join the recession of Egypt, where they were living at the time. You'll find the account in the book of Exodus. Israel was a slave to Egypt. Pharaoh refused to let God's people go, so God sent one plague after another on Egypt. Some of those plagues were financial plagues, including one when Moses told Pharaoh that a murrain, or disease, was going to befall all of Egypt's cattle, donkeys, camels, and sheep. In that day and age, those commodities represented their wealth. That was their money in the bank. When God told Pharaoh what was going to happen to Egypt, He said:

> Behold, the hand of the Lord is upon thy cattle which is in the field, upon the horses, upon the asses, upon the camels, upon the oxen, and upon the sheep: there shall be a very grievous murrain. And the Lord shall sever between the cattle of Israel and the cattle of Egypt: and there shall nothing die of all that is the children's of Israel.
>
> Exod. 9:3-4

In essence, God told Pharaoh, "I'm going to draw a line between you and Israel. Not one of its sheep, not one of its cattle, not one of its possessions is going to die." And that's exactly what happened. While the world was enduring a financial plague, God protected His people.

Later on, another plague came along—this time a plague of hail. Once again, God promised protection for His people. He told Egypt, "When this hail falls, anything that might have survived the last plague is going to be killed—any sheep, goats or anything still alive is going to be killed. You're going to lose financially again—but not My people the Israelites. I'm going to protect their possessions from this hail" (Exod. 9:18-21, paraphrased). Again, that's exactly what happened:

> And the hail smote throughout all the land of Egypt all that was in the field, both man and beast; and the hail smote every herb of the field, and brake every tree of the field. Only in the land of Goshen, where the children of Israel were, was there no hail.
>
> Exod. 9:25-26

So you see there *is* scriptural precedent for believers being recession-proof. There's precedent for you to watch the world struggle financially while you do not endure the same struggles. In fact, you are going to see in our twenty-eight-day challenge that there is even scriptural precedent for your being in a place where God increases you while the world around you is decreasing.

This is not about God loving you more than anyone else; it is simply about which side you are on and which system you have chosen to operate in—God's system or the world's system. God has set out certain specific requirements for you to follow if you want to walk in His blessings. That's what we're going to study during the next twenty-eight days. His Word is clear, and He offers a practical strategy to help you thrive and prosper—even in tough economic times. His heart is to keep recession out of your house and to cause wealth and riches to be in your house instead. His plan—if you follow it—will get you out of the world's banking system and allow Him to be your Banker. This is not about how you can amass riches for yourself; true prosperity is having the ability to help others. God wants to position you so that He can bless you to be a greater blessing to the world around you.

Are you ready to get started? I encourage you to press through and make a commitment to finish the twenty-eight-day challenge. The only thing you have to lose is your recession.

Day 2

DOES GOD WANT YOU TO BE PROSPEROUS?

W E MUST BEGIN OUR JOURNEY TO BECOMING RECESSION-proof by answering once and for all these questions: Does God even care about my financial well-being? Does He want me to be prosperous, and if so, why? Before we answer, consider the following stories. Mike Burns liked working in his yard because he found it relaxing. There was something about getting out in the fresh air and getting his hands dirty that rejuvenated him. He remembered working in his grandfather's garden when he was a boy, and those were pleasant memories. Now he could work in his own garden. Some might think it strange to see a newly minted deca-millionaire outside in work clothes, but Mike did not care. He did not get where he was by forgetting the simpler things in life. He got there by obeying God's Word. He remembered walking into Encounter Christian Center as a man who barely had enough to feed his family. That's where he heard Pastor Richardson preach on tithes and offerings. He questioned the doctrine at the time, not because it was not in the Bible—he couldn't argue that—but because it seemed unrealistic. If he were to give God the first 10 percent of everything he made, there would not be enough left to provide for his own family. He had heard the whispers of those who claimed the pastor was only preaching that message to get rich, and he almost allowed himself to believe it.

 Does God even care about my financial well-being? Does He want me to be prosperous, and if so, why?

However, he could not get away from the fact that what the pastor taught was found in the Bible. He couldn't get out of his head that it was God, not his pastor, who said these things. God was the One who promised to have his "barns filled with plenty" and give him "overflowing success" in his career. Most of all, there was something planted in his heart letting him know that God wanted to give money to him. For some reason, he felt God was saying that the money would not be just for his own needs and desires. God was saying He needed Mike to be a "money missionary," who would finance the preaching of the gospel throughout the earth and show the love of God to those in need around him.

Mike began to work the kingdom principles revealed to him in the Bible. It took some time and some patience, but after a while, he began to see God do what He promised. Mike's Web company absolutely took off! As he learned to hear from God and obey His direction, he found that God is the best Businessman who ever was. Mike began to see that his pastor didn't preach about financial prosperity because he was trying to rob people of their money; he was preaching it because it is in God's Word. Mike smiled as he thought about what his pastor said: "When people act on God's Word, it works."

Crystal fell across her bed exhausted. She had just gotten the babies into bed, and after some coaxing, they finally stayed there and fell asleep. Being a single mother was difficult, and it was especially difficult raising two boys. They were so full of energy! She loved them very much. Their father had no idea what he was missing by not being part of their lives. He also had no idea what child support was. Crystal hated to report him to the authorities, but she had no choice. Didn't Pastor Richardson quote from the Bible that very Sunday, "A man who won't take care of his own is worse than an infidel"? Anyway, she needed the money. The eviction notice on her door made that clear. She had no idea what to do. She was already working two jobs. Tears ran down her face as she cried herself to sleep.

Pastor Richardson locked the door to his office and turned on his iPod to listen to some praise music. He decided that no matter how he felt, he was going to praise God for the victory, and he raised his hands in worship, even though the bank statements and spreadsheets on his desk tried to make him do otherwise. "Don't wait for the walls to fall!" he often told the congregation. "Shout now!" He'd taught it time and time again. He'd seen it work in the lives of so many of his members. Now the whole church needed it to work. The only way they were going to be able to go forward with building their new sanctuary was if a miracle occurred. Pastor Richardson refused to look down at the financials on his desk as he lifted his voice in thanksgiving to God.

Alex was hopeful. He'd heard great things about the church that he and his family were going to visit. They had been looking for a good church for a while. He was surprised at how hard it was to find what he considered a good church. Either the churches he visited didn't teach the Bible, or they taught that "prosperity gospel" that Alex hated so much. He had a real problem with that type of teaching. Didn't those pastors know that Jesus was poor? Didn't they know that God has called us to suffer in this life, not prosper?

Alex shook his head thinking about his last pastor. *A real follower of Jesus would not drive to church in such a nice car,* he thought to himself. *Where are these ministers getting their money, anyway?* Alex was convinced they were only preaching that message for their personal financial gain. The Bible talked about preachers who were greedy of filthy lucre. These guys must have been whom God was talking about.

Crystal barely made it to church on time for praise and worship, but she was glad she did. She had felt so down this morning and so overwhelmed by her situation, but after joining thousands of other believers in true worship, she felt encouraged. She couldn't believe how hopeful she felt when nothing about her situation had changed.

Pastor Richardson was now preparing to take up the offering. He was teaching from 1 Kings chapter 17 as he shared the story of the widow who was about to have her last meal. God instructed her to financially support Elijah, the prophet of God, and promised that if she did, the Lord would provide for her. She did, and God was faithful to His word.

More than any time in her life, Crystal felt she could relate to this woman—but she couldn't see herself giving in her situation. And there were a thousand reasons why. Pastor Richardson interrupted her list. "Sometimes God will speak to you about giving when you're in a time of need," he said. "God isn't trying to take something from you, but trying to get something to you. If God is dealing with your heart about giving, you should obey Him. If you've got a need, God is probably talking to you about seed!"

Crystal reluctantly searched her heart and was surprised to sense God leading her to give something during the offering. She hesitated and then looked at 1 Kings chapter 17 herself. She read what God did for the widow. She heard the pastor exhorting the people to "give first of all in love, because you love God and want people to be blessed, then give in faith, believing that God will return a harvest to you."

Crystal reached into her purse and grabbed her checkbook, determined to give exactly what God told her to give. Yes, it was all she had to pay toward her rent, but it wouldn't cover it, anyway. She would be a blessing to someone else by helping him or her hear the gospel, and she'd trust God to help her keep her home.

Alex had to admit, he was thoroughly impressed. From the moment they pulled onto the property, he whispered to his wife over and over again, "I think we've found our church home!" He and his family were greeted with smiling faces and welcoming words. During praise and worship, he felt as if he were being taken to the throne room itself! He loved the testimony of a family that had been in the church only one year; they went from being unsaved, living together not married, and generally miserable, to a place where they were born-again, happily married, and mature enough in Christ to be starting a small group in their home. It was very emotional. Even Alex's wife began to cry as the couple shared their story with tears welling up in their eyes. *This*, he thought, *is how church should be.*

He wasn't thrilled with the offering teaching, though; it sounded too close to a prosperity teaching. However, he was willing to overlook that and give the pastor a chance—that is, until he announced the title of his message: "Lenders and Not Borrowers." Alex quickly felt the anger rising inside him. He turned to his wife and said loud enough for everyone around him to hear, "Another prosperity preacher. What a crook!" Alex steamed as Pastor Richardson went through Scripture after Scripture revealing God's desire to prosper His people financially and how they needed to cooperate with Him not only by giving, but also by properly managing the money God gave them. It was all too much for Alex. As dozens of people responded to the altar call given for those who desired to receive Jesus or rededicate their lives to Him, Alex grabbed his family and hastily exited the church.

Wow, what a great message! Mike thought. No matter how many times he heard a message about finances, he loved it. He knew messages like this had helped him to get out of debt and into position to be a greater blessing. He also loved to see so many people give their lives to Jesus even on a Sunday when the message was about money! It would surprise him more if he didn't see this scene on Sunday morning because he had seen it played out again and again.

After the service was over, he approached Pastor Richardson with excitement bubbling up inside him. He had waited so long for this day! He had declared years before to the pastor that one day he was going to give $1 million to the church. Of course, he barely had enough to get by on then, but pastor didn't discourage him. He quoted to him what the Bible teaches in Mark 11:23, that we have what we say. Little did pastor know that day was here.

Pastor Richardson had just finished talking with a young couple at the back of the church. He was exhausted from the long day, but pleased that God had used him. As he turned to head toward his office, he noticed Mike Burns walking toward him. He smiled to himself, remembering how much Mike had grown. He was a walking testimony of what happens when a person follows God's financial principles.

"Hey, Mike, it's good to see you," he said, shaking hands.

"Great message today, Pastor," said Mike. "I promised you something a few years back." He reached into his coat pocket and pulled out a check. "This is for the new building," he said, handing the check to his pastor.

"God bless you, Mike," Pastor Richardson said with a smile, "and may you receive an abundant return." He turned to give the check to an usher near him, who quickly placed it in an offering envelope.

"Pastor, I think you may want to look at this one," Mike said.

Pastor Richardson looked at Mike and asked for the check back from the usher. When he opened it, he almost dropped it. "Hallelujah!" he shouted. People turned to look and saw their pastor dancing up the aisle giving God glory. Others began to join him, not knowing why he was rejoicing so, but enjoying it just the same. Mike smiled and joined in, too. Today was the day God had promised him years ago, and there was a lot to rejoice about.

Alex was still fuming as he drove home. He turned on his favorite Christian radio station just in time to hear a preacher bashing the prosperity message, even calling out preachers by name. Alex enthusiastically said, "Amen!" to the statement that "Preachers shouldn't be preaching about money. They should only talk about 'taking up the cross of Christ.'"

"He's got that right," Alex muttered. "We'll never go back to that church!"

His wife nodded her head at him and turned to look out the window sadly.

Crystal got her sons situated in the backseat. She felt so encouraged now. She was entirely confident that whatever God had to do,

He would meet her need. As she opened her car doors, she saw Mike Burns coming over to say hello.

"Hi, Crystal!" he called to her.

"Hi, Mike," she answered. "How's Tara doing?"

"She's great," Mike replied. "Crystal, as I was getting in my car, God told me to come talk to you. Are you in some type of financial bind?"

Crystal's knees almost buckled. Somehow she kept her composure, thinking she should get an Oscar for her performance. Slowly she told Mike her situation. Mike nodded as he listened, then pulled out his checkbook, wrote out a check, and handed it to Crystal.

"Crystal, I believe God wants Tara and me to help you," he said, putting the check into her hand. Tears ran down Crystal's face as she saw the numbers on the check. It was exactly double what she needed to pay her rent.

"Thank You, God," she whispered. "And thank you, Mike."

"God loves you, Crystal. Enjoy the blessing."

As Mike got behind the wheel of his new sports car, he thought, *I always wanted a car like this, but I have to say, nothing compares to being able to bless someone else when they need it. The Bible was right. "It is more blessed to give than to receive"* (Acts 20:35).

Day 3

WHAT DOES THE
BIBLE SAY?

I T WAS A THURSDAY AFTERNOON, AND A GUEST MINISTER AT OUR
church asked if I had read an article in *Time* magazine titled
"Does God Want You to Be Rich?"[1] As he described the content,
the article piqued my interest, and I looked for it online. I soon found
myself staring at a computer screen engrossed in one of the more
comprehensive, if somewhat misguided, secular articles on what has
been tagged the "prosperity gospel."

Why was I so interested? Let me tell you a little about myself. I
am a preacher's son who received the call to ministry at the age of
seventeen. I had no interest in ministry at the time. I had received a
full scholarship to a well-respected university and planned on taking

it. Instead, the Lord led me to attend a small, unaccredited ministry school. I had learned enough about the things of God to know that following His plan was the best course I could take in life.

The most memorable and important lesson I learned at that school was similar to what my own father taught in my home church: The Bible should be the final authority in your life. That simply meant that what the Bible says should form your views about every area of life. Being a pretty logical thinker, that concept made sense to me. For a Christian, the Bible is the manual for living. Everything we know about Jesus Christ and the things of God comes from it. Without it, there is no Christianity.

Furthermore, Jesus Himself said, "Man shall not live by bread alone, but by every word of God" (Luke 4:4). Some say that the Bible was not meant to be taken literally. My response to that is, "Somebody should have told Jesus." He purposely lived His life by what the Old Testament had to say about living for God. This revelation about the Bible has served me well throughout my life and ministry, as it has so many others.

You must be thinking that I haven't answered the question. Why was I so interested in that magazine article? Here's the kicker: The school I attended is called Rhema Bible Training Center, the creation of one Kenneth E. Hagin. Reverend Hagin's life has impacted literally millions of others throughout the world. Although not as well-known as Billy Graham, his life was no less fruitful for God than the great evangelist. Kenneth Hagin is mostly known for his teachings on the subject of faith. Hs teachings on faith and prosperity have greatly influenced the lives of such men and women of God as Kenneth Copeland, the late John Osteen, Creflo Dollar, Joyce Meyer, and many more.

I've been raised hearing the so-called prosperity gospel all my life. Some would say I'm a son of the so-called prosperity gospel. So here I am, a man who has been taught to form my beliefs solely on what the Bible teaches, and a man who has personally sat under the ministry of many of the most prominent prosperity gospel preachers of this day, reading another article on the subject. It had been my belief for a number of years that those criticizing the message had never really bothered to sit and actually study it. I felt this way because so many things people were saying about it led me to wonder, *Who on earth is preaching that?* There was a lack of true research done on the subject by those so quick to deride it.

This article, however, was not like any other I'd read. True, it contained some of the more common incorrect statements I'd read before, such as that prosperity is an American doctrine, and it had the same silly insinuations that anyone preaching it is only doing so to somehow enrich themselves. But it also was at least willing to look at the other side of the issue, that maybe the Bible actually taught what these ministers were teaching, that this was not just some made-up doctrine sweeping the country, but that maybe these ministers were just doing what the Bible said—"Preach the Word"— versus preaching what fits man's opinion or makes them feel religiously comfortable.

 Is God's Word definitive in its teachings, or does it leave us to figure it out on our own?

Unfortunately, the article predictably veered toward the same misinformed conclusion as so many others. That in itself was not necessarily a big deal, as I've seen it before. However, one statement jumped out at me above all else, and it is because of this statement that I am writing this book: "Scripture is not definitive when it comes to faith and income."[2] Following this statement was a similar one: "So the Bible leaves plenty of room for a discussion on the role, positive or negative, that money should play in the lives of believers."[3]

After reading these two statements, I decided it was time to set the record straight. What does the Bible really have to say about this matter? Is God's Word definitive in its teachings, or does it leave us to figure it out on our own? Does the Bible teach that God wants you to be rich or not? That is why I wrote this book—to answer those questions. During the twenty-eight-day challenge, you will find out the answers for yourself.

I once heard a story about a legendary football coach whose team was in a championship game. His team was not playing well, and at halftime, the coach grabbed a football and lifted it in the air in front of the team. He said, "This is a football," and began to explain the sport of football beginning with the basics of the sport. There is no better way for me to begin this study than to say, "This is a Bible!" So let's start with the basics by learning the rules of Bible interpretation.

Rule #1: Only God's interpretation matters. "Study to shew thyself approved unto God, a workman that needeth not to be ashamed, rightly dividing the word of truth" (2 Tim. 2:15).

There are a few things that we need to establish about the Bible. It teaches in 2 Tim. 3:16 (as well as 2 Pet. 1:21, among other places) that every bit of it is God-breathed, or straight from the mouth of God. Some say men wrote the Bible, but the Bible teaches clearly that God used men to write out His thoughts in the same way that an executive might dictate a letter to his or her secretary. Although the secretary may have physically produced the letter, clearly the letter came from the executive. There are numerous proofs that the Bible is divinely inspired, but that is not the topic of this book. (See the works of Josh McDowell and many other apologists for more on this topic.)

Jesus used the Bible as the final authority in His life when He rejected Satan's temptations on the basis of, "It is written." He was saying, in essence, that His beliefs and behavior were formed based on what God has said in His written Word more so than on anything else, even His mind and His body. His teachings later prove that God expects those who serve Him to treat His Word, the Bible, as the foundation of their beliefs and actions. (We've already addressed the question "Should the Bible be taken literally?" Jesus took it literally, as did Peter, John, and Paul.)

Some may ask, "How can we do that when there are so many ways that one can interpret Scripture?" Undoubtedly, you've heard people use terms like, "That's your interpretation," or, "My interpretation of that is . . . ." The problem with such statements is they imply that Scripture is open to individual interpretations. Therefore, no interpretation of Scripture can really be proved as right or wrong when the Bible explicitly teaches differently. The Bible in 2 Tim. 2:15 teaches us to do our homework, to study Scripture thoroughly so as to rightly divide or interpret it. The fact that Scripture can be rightly divided means that it can be wrongly divided. It means that every Scripture has a right interpretation—a certain thought (or thoughts) that God was communicating—and every other interpretation is wrong. Two plus two equals four; any answer you give to this simple math problem besides four is wrong. Such is the way of this world; there is right, and then there is wrong. This applies to Bible interpretation. This means that the only interpretation that matters is God's interpretation, and you get that by studying His Word. There is no place for man's interpretation. The following Scripture proves this point definitively: "Knowing this first, that no prophecy of the scripture is of any private interpretation. For the prophecy came not in old time by the will of man: but holy men of God spake as they were moved by the Holy Ghost" (2 Pet. 2:20-21).

Rule #2: Interpret Scripture in the light of other Scripture. So how do we study the Bible? What will help us to get an understanding of what God was really saying in each Scripture? It's quite simple, really: When you read a Scripture, you need to study it in context. Don't focus only on the Scripture, but on the Scriptures before and after it, the chapter it is in, the chapters preceding and following it, the book of the Bible it is in, whether it is in the Old or New Testament, and, ultimately, the Scripture in the context of the entire Bible itself. You will never see God contradict Himself in Scripture. If you think you have found a contradiction, you have not studied it enough. This is one of the reasons we know it is divinely inspired. God used approximately fifty authors from different time periods. Most of them did not know each other, and many of them had not read each other's writings. God used them to tell the same story (the story of Jesus) without contradiction.

The best example of this is the Bible's many prophecies concerning the coming Messiah. There are more than one hundred prophecies in the Old Testament alone about the Messiah. Any self-respecting historian will tell you that these books were clearly written before Jesus was born. However, they were extremely accurate in describing the details of His life, from where He would be born, to what He would say, to how He would die, and more. The mathematical odds of all these prophecies coming true in the life of one man are astronomical (more than 1 trillion to one). Yet they did all come to pass in the life of a Man named Jesus!

"In the mouth of two or three witnesses shall every word be established" (2 Cor. 13:1). Paul, the apostle, makes mention of another principle in 2 Cor. 13:1 that will help us to properly interpret the Bible. He uses this principle in a slightly different way in this context, but he quotes a method that God gave men to employ in order to establish when a given testimony was truthful or not. Using this God-given principle means simply checking the interpretation you believe is right by seeing if you can find other Scripture to corroborate your findings (of course, studying them in context). If you can locate a second and a third witness (many times, as we'll see in the coming days, God gives many more than three), then you have rightly divided what God was saying in the Scripture you are studying.

Something else that will help you in your study is to remember that the English translations we have of the Bible are just that, translations. Sometimes to get the full meaning of a Scripture, you need to look up the original Hebrew (Old Testament) or Greek (New Testament) words used and examine their meanings and other uses. Study helps such as *Strong's Exhaustive Concordance of the Bible* and Vine's Expository dictionaries as well as many Bible software programs help make this an easy thing to do.

Rule #3: Don't reject what the Bible says. "And he said unto them, Full well ye reject the commandment of God, that ye may keep your own tradition. Making the word of God of none effect through your tradition, which ye have delivered: and many such like things do ye" (Mark 7:9, 13).

A common error made by Christians, especially ministers, is that we will reject what the Bible says because it does not appear to be consistent with our long-held beliefs. We can be quick to forget that our beliefs are to be formed by what the Bible says and nothing else. This problem is especially an issue when one talks about the prosperity message. Either ministers are ignorant of what the Bible says on the issue (and I mean the entire Bible), or they reject Scriptures because they are not consistent with their thinking about God and the Christian life. Sometimes it is because of preconceived ideas about God that they received from other ministers of the gospel that they are ignorant about what the Bible says on the issue. They never truly approach the Word of God or teaching of the Word about prosperity with an open heart; instead, they quickly say, "That's just a get-rich-quick gospel," or, "They're teaching that getting rich is the goal of Christian life," or, "He's just trying to enrich himself," or other such statements.

This attitude is exactly what Jesus dealt with in His encounters with the Pharisees. He brought a revelation about God as a Father, a good God who was not just a Judge, but who loves His people. They rejected it. Some today still struggle with this view of God that Jesus Himself introduced. He brought understanding concerning the Messiah, and they rejected it. Everything He did and taught was entirely consistent with the law they claimed to be following, yet because they did not know their own law, they rejected Him.

Let us not be like the Pharisees. Let's have an open heart when we approach the Bible, not like the people of Matthew chapter 13 who had dull ears and closed eyes to the words of God. Instead, let us be like the Bereans in Acts 17:10-11 who heard Paul speak and then daily searched the Scriptures and so saw that what was preached, although it was new to them, was true. Prov. 1:5 teaches, "A wise man will hear, and will increase learning." During our twenty-eight-day challenge—and beyond—let us be like the wise man, who is open to God's thoughts and God's ways as revealed in the Bible and will exalt them above the ideals (even religious) of others and ourselves.

Day 4

PROOFS FROM THE BIBLE

I WANT YOU TO SEE THAT WHAT WE STUDIED YESTERDAY IS NOT something I made up. There are proofs throughout the Old and New Testaments that show God's desire is for you to prosper financially and otherwise. Today we're going to cover just a handful of them, but you can find many more in the appendix of this book as well as throughout the Bible. As you read these verses, ask yourself what the Bible is saying.

Abram: "Now the Lord had said unto Abram, Get thee out of thy country, and from thy kindred, and from thy father's house, unto a land that I will shew thee: And I will make of thee a great nation, and I will bless thee, and make thy name great; and thou shalt be a blessing. . . . And the Lord hath blessed my master greatly; and he is become great: and he hath given him flocks, and herds, and silver, and gold, and menservants, and maidservants, and camels, and asses" (Gen. 12:1-2; 24:35).

Isaac: "Then Isaac sowed in that land, and received in the same year an hundredfold: and the Lord blessed him. And the man waxed great, and went forward, and grew until he became very great: For he had possession of flocks, and possession of herds, and great store of servants: and the Philistines envied him. And Abimelech said unto Isaac, Go from us; for thou art much mightier than we" (Gen. 26:12-14, 16).

Jacob: "And he said unto him, Thou knowest how I have served thee, and how thy cattle was with me. For it was little which thou hadst before I came, and it is now increased unto a multitude; and the Lord hath blessed thee since my coming. . . . And the man increased exceedingly, and had much cattle, and maidservants, and menservants, and camels, and asses. . . . Thus God hath taken away the cattle of your father, and given them to me" (Gen. 30:29-30, 43; 31:9).

Joseph: "Thou shalt be over my house, and according unto thy word shall all my people be ruled: only in the throne will I be greater than thou. And Pharaoh said unto Joseph, See, I have set thee over all the land of Egypt. And Pharaoh took off his ring from his hand, and put it upon Joseph's hand, and arrayed him in vestures of fine linen, and put a gold chain about his neck; And he made him to ride in the second chariot which he had; and they cried before him, Bow the knee: and he made him ruler over all the land of Egypt" (Gen. 41:40-43).

Moses and the children of Israel: "And the children of Israel did according to the word of Moses; and they borrowed of the Egyptians jewels of silver, and jewels of gold, and raiment: And the Lord gave the people favour in the sight of the Egyptians, so that they lent unto them such things as they required. And they spoiled the Egyptians" (Exod. 12:35-36).

You: "For the Lord thy God bringeth thee into a good land, a land of brooks of water, of fountains and depths that spring out of valleys and hills; a land of wheat, and barley, and vines, and fig trees, and pomegranates; a land of oil olive, and honey; a land wherein thou shalt eat bread without scarceness, thou shalt not lack any thing in it; a land whose stones are iron, and out of whose hills thou mayest dig brass. When thou hast eaten and art full, then thou shalt bless the Lord thy God for the good land which he hath given thee" (Deut. 8:7-10).

Solomon: "So king Solomon exceeded all the kings of the earth for riches and for wisdom. And all the earth sought to Solomon, to hear his wisdom, which God had put in his heart. And they brought every man his present, vessels of silver, and vessels of gold, and garments, and armour, and spices, horses, and mules, a rate year by year" (1 Kings 10:23-25).

Job: "So the Lord blessed the latter end of Job more than his beginning: for he had fourteen thousand sheep, and six thousand camels, and a thousand yoke of oxen, and a thousand she asses" (Job 42:12).

 If you say that God does not desire to prosper His people financially, you would have to ignore and discount these and many other Scriptures found throughout the Bible.

You: "Christ hath redeemed us from the curse of the law. . . . That the blessing of Abraham might come on the Gentiles through Jesus Christ; that we might receive the promise of the Spirit through faith" (Gal. 3:13-14).

You: "Beloved, I wish above all things that thou mayest prosper and be in health, even as thy soul prospereth" (3 John 1:2). The original Greek says "in all things."

You: "And Jesus answered and said, Verily I say unto you, There is no man that hath left house, or brethren, or sisters, or father, or mother, or wife, or children, or lands, for my sake, and the gospel's, but he shall receive an hundredfold now in this time, houses, and brethren, and sisters, and mothers, and children, and lands, with persecutions; and in the world to come eternal life" (Mark 10:29-30).

If you say that God does not desire to prosper His people financially, you would have to ignore and discount these and many other Scriptures found throughout the Bible. According to Mal. 3:6 and Heb. 13:8, God does not change. His will for man at one time in history is the same as it is today or in the future. If it was true for Abraham, Isaac, Jacob, Joseph, Moses, Solomon, and Job, it is true today for you.

Hopefully after you've read these proofs, you agree that it is completely within God's will to want to prosper you financially. If you're like some Christians, however, a question may still remain in your mind: What about preachers; should preachers have money? The world has an answer to that, but they don't really know what the Bible teaches. As Christians, we do know the Bible, so let's study this and make a decision to agree with God's Word. We understand what people think, but let's see what God thinks about this subject.

> And the Lord spake unto Aaron, Thou shalt have no inheritance in their land, neither shalt thou have any part among them: I am thy part and thine inheritance among the children of Israel. And, behold, I have given the children of Levi all the tenth in Israel for an inheritance, for their service which they serve, even the service of the tabernacle of the congregation. But the tithes of the children of Israel, which they offer as an heave offering unto the Lord, I have given to the Levites to inherit: therefore I have said unto them, Among the children of Israel they shall have no inheritance.
>
> Num. 18:20-21, 24

And that we should bring the firstfruits of our dough, and our offerings, and the fruit of all manner of trees, of wine and of oil, unto the priests, to the chambers of the house of our God; and the tithes of our ground unto the Levites, that the same Levites might have the tithes in all the cities of our tillage.

Neh. 10:37

Under the law, it was the will of God that priests be provided for, and that happened through the tithe of the people. But you may say, "Pastor, I don't live in ancient Israel, and we no longer take goats out and sacrifice them unto the Lord. I want to know what the Bible has to say about this area for today."

There is no better person to talk about this in the Bible than Paul. In 1 Cor. 9:1-3, he tackles the issue of preachers and money.

Am I not an apostle? am I not free? have I not seen Jesus Christ our Lord? are not ye my work in the Lord? If I be not an apostle unto others, yet doubtless I am to you: for the seal of mine apostleship are ye in the Lord. Mine answer to them that do examine me is this.

Notice that people were criticizing Paul and his ministry. Jesus said, "They hated me, so they will hate you. They persecuted me, so they're going to persecute you" (Matt. 23:34-36, paraphrased). Paul, the greatest of the apostles, the most productive individual during his time, was being criticized and persecuted. Here's what he says in response:

Have we not power to eat and to drink? Have we not power to lead about a sister, a wife, as well as other apostles, and as the brethren of the Lord, and Cephas? Or I only and Barnabas, have not we power to forbear working? Who goeth a warfare any time at his own charges? who planteth a vineyard, and eateth not of the fruit thereof? or who feedeth a flock, and eateth not of the milk of the flock?

1 Cor. 9:4-7

Notice three key terms—warfare, planteth, and feedeth. When he mentions them, he's talking about the ministry. He's saying, "As I go forth and minister unto you, that is going into warfare. I'm being a soldier. I am putting myself at risk to minister to you. As I minister unto you, I'm planting a vineyard. I'm going out under the hot sun, and I'm taking the seed of the Word of God, and I'm sowing it in your hearts. As I minister unto you, I'm feeding you like a shepherd feeds the flock; I'm going forth and gathering the food that you need and bringing it unto you so that you can prosper."

Some people have the mentality that ministry is easy. They think all the preacher does is get up on Sunday and talk for an hour, get up on Wednesday and talk for an hour, and go home for the rest of the week and watch television. I am sorry; that is not the case.

Paul said, "Let the elders that rule well be counted worthy of double honour" (1 Tim. 5:17). The words "counted worthy" do not mean, "He did such a good job that he really deserves twice what he makes." That's not what Paul is saying here. The word *honour* here means "money paid." It means "price." In other words, Paul is saying that those elders who are ruling well, who are productive, who are doing a good job of getting people born again and training up believers and taking care of them, the leaders who are causing the kingdom of God to prosper, they're worthy. Let them be counted worthy, and let them be paid double their salary.

Still not convinced? Do you still think Paul is just talking about honoring someone? Look at verse 18. "For the scripture saith, thou shalt not muzzle the ox that treadeth out the corn. And, the labourer is worthy of his reward." This Scripture is not talking about standing up and giving him honor or having a special night for the pastor or putting a plaque up in the lobby for the preacher. In fact, let's double up and put up two plaques! The man doesn't have any clothes or money, but you're going to put up a plaque for him?

No, Paul is telling us to make sure that the ones who rule well and are bearing fruit for the kingdom are rewarded financially. It doesn't say anything about a plaque. God says, "If they rule well, double their salary. Give them double for their trouble. As far as God is concerned, a faithful preacher or teacher of the Word should be more than taken care of financially. There is nothing wrong with a man of God having more than enough. As far as God is concerned, preachers should have money.

Tomorrow we're going to study what true prosperity is. (You may be surprised.)

Day 5

TRUE PROSPERITY

THESE ARE JUST TWO OF THE MANY SCRIPTURE PASSAGES that describe what the real prosperity message is:

> But seek ye first the kingdom of God, and his righteousness; and all these things shall be added unto you.
>
> Matt. 6:33

> And God is able to make all grace (every favor and earthly blessing) come to you in abundance, so that you may always and under all circumstances and whatever the need be self-sufficient [possessing enough to require no aid or support and furnished in abundance for every good work and charitable donation].... Thus you will be enriched in all things and in every way, so that

you can be generous, and [your generosity as it is] administered
by us will bring forth thanksgiving to God.

2 Cor. 9:8, 11 AMP

Love. Blessed to be a blessing. Money with a mission. These are
words and statements that accurately describe true prosperity. What
some refer to in a derogatory manner as the "prosperity message" is
really a message about love. True prosperity is God so loving us that
He gave His Son to us so that we could have eternal life. True prosperity is God so loving us that He said He would give good things to
us (see Matt. 7:7-11). True prosperity is God so loving us that Rom.
8:32 teaches that if He spared not His son for us, how could He not
with Him freely give us all things?

 True prosperity is learning to live not in
order to get, but to give, as Eph. 4:28 reveals
to us.

True prosperity is God so loving us that He serves as Jehovah
Jireh—God the Provider—in our lives so that we do not need to have
marriages cracking under the strain of financial pressure. True prosperity is God so loving us that we do not have to send our kids into the
spiritual danger zones of some of today's public schools, that we do
not have to depend on the government for food, shelter, or support in
our latter years. True prosperity is God so loving us that He provides
us with riches and wealth for us to enjoy (see 1 Tim. 6:17; Eccles. 5:18-
20). All while we enjoy the real treasure of knowing Him, loving Him,
seeking Him, and serving Him.

True prosperity is about being blessed so that we can be a blessing,
as is taught in 2 Cor. 9:8, 11. True prosperity is learning to live not in
order to get, but to give, as Eph. 4:28 reveals to us. True prosperity is

understanding that the main reason God desires to get money to us is to get money through us. It is understanding that God desires to use us as He did the disciples in John chapter 6 when He had them distribute the five loaves and two fishes, when He had them act as distribution centers for Him to do good works in the financial arena. True prosperity is, as 1 Tim. 6:18-19 teaches us, to remember to be rich in good works, ready to communicate, willing to distribute. True prosperity is to be the liberal soul of Prov. 11:24, the one with a bountiful eye in Prov. 22:9 (after all, one cannot give what one does not have), the one whose deeds of giving last forever, such as those of the man in Psalm 112.

Our desire is to be one who has laid up treasure in heaven as Jesus instructed us in Matt. 6:20. Our goal is to be like Jesus, to prove the sincerity of our love by our abundant giving (see 2 Cor. 8:7-8). We desire to be used by God to help the poor, downtrodden, broken, and lacking. We desire to be the men spoken of in Luke 6:38 who give into the bosom of another, and are thus used as an instrument of God to show His love to the poor, downtrodden, broken, and lacking.

True prosperity is about money with a mission. It is following the example of those in the church of Philippi, who helped finance the preaching of the gospel in Paul's ministry, and the example of Gaius from 3 John, whose giving made him a fellow-helper in the gospel. True prosperity is about seeking first the building of God's kingdom through giving so that others can hear the same life-changing message that we did about Jesus. True prosperity is about giving so that people can hear the message as many times as they need to before it registers in their heart and they see the truth about Jesus. (How many times did you have to hear it before you chose to receive Him?) True prosperity is about following Paul's example and presenting the Good News in as many ways as we can to get the world's attention.

No longer can we simply sit by and allow Satan's agenda, financed by the wealth of the wicked, to reign supreme in our music, movies, magazines, schools, establishments, government, media, and, ultimately, culture. It is time we allow God to prosper us so that we can take back these arenas and use every possible tool to save as many as we can.

God's will is clearly stated in Matthew 24:14—the Great Commission: "And this gospel of the kingdom shall be preached in all the world for a witness unto all nations." This has to be financed. It costs money to minister. As much as we may not like it, money matters in this world and has an impact on how many will hear about Jesus and become the disciples that He desires us to be. How many churches have not been able to grow due to a lack of the necessary funds because their people are struggling in this arena? How many believers overseas would testify that the single biggest impediment to their ministry is the lack of money? How many in this country would say the same?

God's will is that ministries today be like Israel in Moses' time, where Moses actually had to tell the people to stop giving because they had more than enough for the building of the tabernacle. This comes about when God's people as a whole are delivered from the curse of poverty and gain an understanding that God has called them into money ministry, to be stewards over His funds in their lives, and to use those funds as He directs to help build His kingdom. It is naive to think that money doesn't play a role in our mission on this earth. It plays a major role. God wants to enrich His people so that they can bountifully give to His good works throughout the earth. A basic principle of war is that he who has the gold wins. This is part of why God desires to get the wealth of the world into the hands of the just, so that He can reach that same world with the message of His love.

As we reach the end of week 1, hopefully you are beginning to see for yourself what the Bible says about this matter. Should you still not agree for whatever reason, I thank you for reading this far and trust that God will continue to minister to you along these lines. For those who feel that they have a mandate to stop this message, I'd encourage you to remember whom we serve and which Spirit is in us. I'd ask that you operate in love. Remember the words of Gamaliel in Acts chapter 5 when he said, "Refrain from these men, and let them alone: for if this counsel or this work be of men, it will come to nought: but if it be of God, ye cannot overthrow it; lest haply ye be found even to fight against God."

Day 6

GROUP DISCUSSION

Action point: Refuse to participate in recession.
Action Scripture: "Therefore all things whatsoever ye would that men should do to you, do ye even so to them: for this is the law and the prophets" (Matt. 7:12).
Action step: Give something toward someone else's debt cancellation this week.

Questions:

1. What did you read in our study this week that surprised you? That caused you to change how you thought about God and His ways? That motivated you to continue on the twenty-eight-day challenge?

2. Name one reason why God doesn't want you to go through recession.

3. If you had $1 million right now, whom would you help with it? Why?

4. Quote two Scriptures, one from the Old Testament, and one from the New Testament, that prove that God wants you prosperous.

5. Does God love preachers, too? Why or why not?

6. What good could one Christian billionaire do in the world today? Be specific with your answer.

Day 7

REST

T O THINK ABOUT TODAY: AT GROUP DISCUSSION THIS WEEK,
we envisioned all the good things that one Christian with a
billion dollars could do in the world today. If you were that
person, what would you like to do with that money? If there was
nothing stopping you or holding you back, what would you do? Allow
yourself to dream big dreams today. Don't let money or the world's
view of reality stop you from thinking about your answer. Don't
allow yourself to say, "That could never happen because . . . ." Let God
dream big dreams through you today.

Week 2

GOD'S RICHES
IN GLORY

Day 8

The Blessing of the Lord Comes from Heaven

Congratulations. You persevered through week 1 of our twenty-eight-day challenge to recession-proof your house. Last week, we studied about true prosperity and learned that God does, in fact, want us to be prosperous—not just for ourselves, but so that we can be a blessing to those around us. I hope that you, like me, decided to "just say no" to the recession. I hope you've decided not to participate.

Remember: Our goal in recession-proofing our houses is not just to benefit ourselves, but to benefit all those around us—not only our immediate family and friends, but unbelievers across the street and across the globe. The principles I'm teaching you are not to help you expand your personal kingdom, but to help you expand the kingdom of God all over the earth. True prosperity is the ability to help others, and that's the place you want to get to. Once you say, "Not in my house," then you can turn around and help someone else deliver their house from financial ruin.

Let's look at Philippians chapter 4.

> Now ye Philippians know also, that in the beginning of the gospel, when I departed from Macedonia, no church communicated with me as concerning giving and receiving, but ye only. For even in Thessalonica ye sent once and again unto my necessity. Not because I desire a gift: but I desire fruit that may abound to your account. But I have all, and abound: I am full, having received of Epaphroditus the things which were sent from you, an odour of a sweet smell, a sacrifice acceptable, wellpleasing to God. But my God shall supply all your need according to his riches in glory by Christ Jesus. Now unto God and our Father be glory for ever and ever. Amen.
>
> Vv. 15-20

If you want to be recession-proof, this passage gives some wonderful direction for you. Paul was writing here about God's great provision and riches. The word *account* is a banking term, isn't it? This passage also tells us that when we give, it is credited to our account, but that's not the main thing I want you to see here. I want to call attention to verse 18, when Paul said, "I have all, and abound. I am full." *Full* means to be crammed up, to be replete, to be filled up. Paul says, "I'm filled up. In fact, I have an abundance. I have more than I need."

Then he goes on to tell the Philippians that God shall supply all their needs, too, and He'll do it according to His riches in glory. He says, "My God," just to make sure they know whom he is talking about, and then adds, "according to his riches in glory by Christ Jesus." We're not talking about Allah, Buddha, or any other "little g" god. In the Old Testament, there are seven redemptive names for God, and they all describe a different aspect of His character—a different aspect of what He provided for us. One of those names is Jehovah Jireh—the Lord who sees, the One who has prevision and gives you provision.

Paul had provision come his way repeatedly throughout his ministry. I know some people want to say that Paul was poor, and therefore we ought to be poor. They need to read the Bible. Paul made three missionary journeys to the entire known world. Travel costs money, yet he was able to do it. So obviously, the money was available. Paul knew God as Provider. So he said, "And the same God who has been providing for me is going to provide for you. He shall supply all your needs." The word *shall* is the strongest assertion in the English language. God can't say it any stronger than that! It's a kingdom-backed guarantee. The word *supply* here means to satisfy; He is going to satisfy all your need. Not just your mortgage, but also your car note. Not just your car note, but also your child's education. Not just your child's education, but the gallon of milk you need for breakfast tomorrow. All means all.

Then he says how God is going to do that: "According to." Now we're talking about a supply line. Back in World War II, if you had your troops in France and you were trying to head to Russia, you literally had supplies in France and a protected path or roadway to make sure those supplies kept coming to the troops on the other side of the front. The enemy would try to cut off that supply line because if they could do that, the troops would die. They wouldn't get the food they needed or the hardware to fight the war. But I'm here to tell you that Satan can't cut off your supply line—because God already said He'll supply all your need according to His own riches.

The blessing of the Lord is not hindered by the environment that it's in.

If I were going to help you pay off your car loan, I'd have to tap into my savings account to do it. I could pay for only as much of your car loan as is in my account. Paul is saying that God will supply all your need according to His riches. That does not mean according to silver or gold or dollar bills. Paul refers to God's "riches in glory." Those are not ordinary riches. Luke chapter 16 tells us that true riches are God's anointing, His power, His ability, what we simply call His blessing. "The blessing of the Lord makes rich" (Prov. 10:22). The blessing of the Lord is God's endowed power for prosperity and success. God literally clothes you with it. It literally comes on your life as if you're wearing it. When it is on you, it causes you to see financial increase. It makes you a money magnet for God. Money miracles consistently manifest in your life, and whatever you put your hand on—if it's a God idea—prospers.

The blessing of the Lord works no matter what environment it is placed in. The blessing of the Lord is not hindered by the environment that it's in. In fact, it's like special forces that go into an especially hostile territory. You would think that territory would swallow them up—but they're there for a reason, because they're special forces. They have the training and strategy necessary to overcome in that area. That's how the blessing is. It will drop into an area that's hostile to prosperity, a place where there is lack. The blessing will take that area and turn it into a Garden of Eden.

That's what God did for Adam and Eve. He created a beautiful planet, and then put them in the Garden of Eden, which, compared to the rest of the planet, was small. He put that blessing on them because He knew it would help them to expand that garden throughout all the rest of the planet.

Look at Isaac during the time of famine. The Bible says that when everyone else was struggling to eat and drink, the blessing was on Isaac—and he got a hundredfold return. He became so rich that the king said, "Leave our nation." It's the same with Joseph when he was a slave in Potiphar's house. What could be a more negative situation than to be in Egypt as the slave of another man? But that blessing was on him and got to working, and everything he put his hand on prospered until he became number two in that house. Eventually, he became number two in jail, and then number two in the entire nation. That blessing will produce no matter what kind of situation it's placed in.

As long as you have that blessing, as long as you have His riches, everything else is irrelevant. It doesn't matter if the world around you is going through a recession or a depression; the blessing will do its job on behalf of those who have received it.

Where is God the Father right now? We know He's omnipresent, but where is He really right now? He's sitting on His throne in heaven. The Bible says, "Every good gift and every perfect gift is from above, and cometh down from the Father of lights" (James 1:17). So the blessing of the Lord comes from heaven, and it rests on men and women on earth. It is a taste of heaven on earth.

Mal. 3:10-12 is a very familiar Scripture passage:

> Bring ye all the tithes into the storehouse, that there may be
> meat in mine house, and prove me now herewith, saith the Lord

of hosts, if I will not open you the windows of heaven, and pour you out a blessing, that there shall not be room enough to receive it. And I will rebuke the devourer for your sakes, and he shall not destroy the fruits of your ground; neither shall your vine cast her fruit before the time in the field, saith the Lord of hosts. And all nations shall call you blessed: for ye shall be a delightsome land, saith the Lord of hosts.

Notice this Scripture is not dependent on if the economy is doing well. It's not dependent on if a Democrat or a Republican is in office. It's not dependent on any of those things. None of those things has anything to do with your prosperity as a child of God. No, He says you'll reach a place where you have so much you don't have room enough to receive it. Why? Because the blessing of the Lord, God's riches, will be working in your life. Where are those blessings coming from? He says He will open the windows of heaven and pour them out to you.

We've got to go back to believing these things. You can't pay attention to what they're saying on CNN and Fox and what you're reading in *The Wall Street Journal* and your local newspaper. We pray for those in the world, but we also believe God to prosper us so we can help take care of those in the world. We cannot be afraid. We cannot worry or cut back on our giving or obedience—because we have a different Banker. We bank in a different place. We bank at the Bank of Heaven—and there's no recession in heaven. The blessing of the Lord is not going to be impacted by falling stock prices or a credit crisis or by people going into foreclosure because it's coming from heaven. Satan can't touch what's in heaven.

A bank can fail, and it doesn't matter to His riches. It doesn't have any impact on it. Credit could freeze, and it doesn't matter to His riches. Real estate prices can fall, and it doesn't have an impact on His riches. The stock market can crash, and it doesn't have an impact. The world's credit system is going to go through things like this. What we are going through today is not the last time we will see something like this. The system is flawed, and the bank that's based upon it is flawed. Only the Bank of Heaven offers true riches, and only the Banker of heaven—Jesus—can truly be your Provider. God has said that what is in heaven is here on earth for you. There is no recession here for you. That means you can confidently say, "Not in my house!"

Day 9

God the Banker

If you have made the decision to recession-proof your house, you've undoubtedly been bombarded by all the negative reports and bad news coming at you from every direction. From newspapers to the TV to the Internet, the word *recession* is seemingly blasted at us no matter where we turn. This week, our goal is to learn to place our faith in God, not in those reports. Why? Because God is a Banker, and He has all the provisions in the universe. He created them, and they're at His disposal, not Wall Street's disposal.

 God is our Banker, and there is no recession in heaven.

We pray for those in the world, we pray for Wall Street, those who've invested in it, the media, and those who are making decisions that affect all of our lives. We pray for them, but we put our trust in God to prosper us so that we can help take care of those in the world. What we're not going to do is be afraid. We're not going to worry. We're not going to cut back on our giving and on our obedience because of what the world is going through, because we have a different Banker and we bank in a different place. God is our Banker, and there is no recession in heaven.

That is why when the world is struggling to survive, we as believers in God can thrive. That is why it's so beneficial to operate according to a different system, because the world's credit system is going to go through things like what we are experiencing now. Mark my word: This is not the last time you will see something like this. We are seeing bandage solutions for a problem that needs major surgery. The current solutions are not going to work because the system is flawed. We'll study that system more next week, but in the meantime, I want to equip you as a believer so that when the system does fail, you don't go down with it. And you don't have to. God doesn't want you to, and He has prepared a way so that you don't have to. That's because He is a very good Banker who has access to unlimited riches in glory.

That's why you must make the decision to let God be your Banker. I'm not telling you to take your money out of a brick-and-mortar bank down the street and keep it under your mattress. I'm telling you that you have to put your faith in God as your Banker. You must make the decision that ultimately, God is in charge of your finances. That decision is going to have ramifications that we'll see in coming weeks of our study, but for now, I want you to see that choosing God as your Banker allows you to have access to all His riches in glory. His riches are His bank. His bank isn't impacted by current events—not in the least. So when God is your Banker, you are not impacted by them, either. It doesn't matter what happens with the stock market. It doesn't matter what happens with the credit market. It doesn't matter what happens with real estate prices. None of these things matter. God's bank is untouchable. You can deposit and withdraw anytime you need to. Time to get a house? The money is there. Time to get a car? The money is there. Time to build a building? The money is there. Time to go on a missions trip? The money is there. Time to build an orphanage for kids in Africa? The money is there. That bank will never fail.

We've been talking about the condition that the world is in, and how God's bank is not impacted by it. Let's take it a step further. God is going to provide for you no matter what your *personal* financial condition is. The blessing doesn't care who is in financial ruin—the government or your bank account. God's bank is not impacted by either one. Once His blessing shows up, it starts working no matter where. The blessing starts paying off school loans and credit cards that we ran up and had no business running up—and we'll talk about that in a couple of weeks. The blessing comes in and pays off your house, your car, and your children's loans. It shows up and provides enough for you to send Bibles to believers in China or shoes for kids in Costa Rica. God is going to do what He said, no matter what your financial state is—and He does it by using His heavenly resources, which never run out. They're inexhaustible. He is a great Banker who has access to all His riches in glory.

God's riches are inexhaustible because heaven is never in recession. So God never has to cut back on the blessing. You will not hear God mumble, "Gosh, things are rough down there. I'm going to have to give them a little bit less than I intended. I have to spread My blessing around, and there's just not enough of it." You will never hear God say that. He never has to cut back on it. He's got an inexhaustible supply of riches.

Have you ever noticed that some people are not impacted by recession? Bill Gates is not really sweating it right now. Nor is

Warren Buffett. He's out there spending billions of dollars buying stock and saving companies. These people aren't even impacted by what's going on around them. And those are just men. If they're not impacted by it, how about the One who said, "The cattle on a thousand hills are Mine, the silver and gold is Mine"? I'm telling you, God is well-equipped to carry out what He has promised you in His Word. My goal is to help you to take that promise of God that He'll supply all your need and actually have it manifest—show up—and work in your life. I want you to experience God Himself giving you exactly what He said He would and exactly how He said He would: good measure, pressed down, shaken together, and running over (see Luke 6:38). I want you to experience His blessing that will cause you to be made rich in every area of your life, including financially. I want to help you see His promises at work in your life. His blessings come from His riches in glory. They are for you and for all His children. If you had blessings stored up for your children, wouldn't you want them to access them? So why would you not access the blessings that your heavenly Father has stored up for you?

Let's look at how God manifested His blessings—His riches in glory—to one person and how that impacted not only him and his family, but also a large part of the world. The person is Abraham. In Genesis chapter 14, Abram (that was his name then) was about to learn what it meant to have God use him and bless him in a mighty way. His nephew lived in Sodom, which had just lost a war and had all its goods taken, as well as those belonging to neighboring Gomorrah. When Abram heard about this, he knew God's anointing was on his life, and he made a plan. He gathered 318 servants, and they pursued the victorious army that had defeated Sodom and Gomorrah and others. They miraculously defeated that army, and all the goods of Sodom and Gomorrah and the other nations now rightfully belonged to Abram and those with him.

When Melchizedek showed up, Abram gave him 10 percent of all that he'd just received—this uncommon harvest. He gave a tithe off of it because it was rightfully his. When the king of Sodom told Abram to take the rest, Abram said, "No, I'm not even going to take a thread or a shoelace of this because I've sworn to God I'm not going to do that. I made a vow to God because I don't want any man to be able to say he made Abram rich" (Gen. 14:23, paraphrased). So Abram took the other 90 percent, which was rightfully his as the spoils of war, and he fulfilled his pledge to God and he sowed it. He sowed what he could have kept. He sowed it all—90 percent.

It's no wonder that chapter 15 opens with extraordinary events. Surely, all these events were fresh in Abram's memory when we read, "After these things the word of the Lord came unto Abram in a vision" (v. 1). Don't you wonder what Abram was thinking after this great victory? Was he concerned about safety for himself and his men? Maybe he was thinking, *Man, I just gave away a whole lot of money. I could have used that to feed these men. I've got a lot of financial needs coming up the first of the month. Did I do the right thing?*

That's when he received an e-mail from the Lord—in the form of a vision. "Fear not, Abram" (v. 1). Don't be afraid, Abram. You don't need to be concerned about anything. Why? "I am thy shield" (v. 1). What is a shield used for? Protection. When a shield is properly used, you have to get through the shield to get to the person wielding the shield. So God was telling Abram not just who He is, but what He would provide for him. "I'm your shield. I'm going to provide protection for you. Anyone who comes at you has to get past Me to get to you."

Psalm 91 tells us that God's truth is our shield and our buckler. Eph. 6:16 says the shield of faith will quench all the fiery darts of the wicked. That would include the assignments of the enemy against our finances. God is our shield. Satan hasn't figured out how to get around Him yet, and he never will.

God had more to say to Abram. "I am thy exceeding great reward" (v. 1). Not just a reward, not just a great reward, but an exceeding great reward. If He had just said, "I'm your reward," coming from God Himself, that would have meant something. But God supersized it and said, "I am your exceeding great reward." The Amplified Bible says, "I'm your abundant compensation." Now, why would someone get a reward or an abundant compensation? Because they've done something good. If you're getting compensated, it's because you've done some work.

Do you see what it means to let God be your Banker? Abram made a choice to do that. His actions were contrary to everything the world would say was right, but he had already begun to see what it was like to do business with God. He did things God's way. He gave the tithe and offering, which we'll study more in coming days, and refused to take goods the wrong way. God rewarded him. In fact, notice that He actually calls Himself "the reward." He says, "*I* am your reward." He didn't just say, "I'm your reward"; he says, "I'm your great reward." There's a difference between having a thousand-dollar reward for giving information about someone who's committed a crime and a million-dollar reward. One is a reward, and the other is a great reward.

But God didn't stop there. He said, "I am your exceeding great reward." When you talk about exceeding, you're talking about going beyond a supposed limit. Now you're talking about something that is limitless. Remember what Paul said about God in Eph. 3:20. He "is able to do exceeding abundantly above all that we ask or think, according to the power that worketh in us." He's able to do exceedingly above—beyond the limit. God was telling Abram, "I am a limitless, great reward for you. I am your Bank. I am your Source." Just as He said that He Himself was Abram's shield, He said He Himself was Abram's exceeding great reward. He would be Abram's Provider, and what He'd provide would be exceeding and great.

Abram really got hold of that because in the next verse, he said, "Lord, what will You give me?" That's not arrogant or selfish. He was responding to what God had just told him. God was showing Abram what role He would play in his life from that point on.

God desires to play the same role in your life as well.

Day 10

God Makes
Provision for Us

AS A MINISTRY, WE ARE PLANNING TO BUILD A NEW BUILDING. The president of a bank came to see us recently, and as we told him what we needed, his reply was always the same: "That's fine. We can do that. We don't have to worry about that. Yes, yes, that's fine." Now, if the president of the bank says it, then you know all the resources of that bank—whatever you need—are there. How about when your heavenly Father is the Bank? How about when He's already made a pledge to you that He's going to provide for your needs, that He's going to be the One who takes care of you, that He's going to be the One who causes you to have exceeding great rewards?

Consider this promise that God made to Job—because it is a promise for you, too.

> If thou return to the Almighty, thou shalt be built up, thou shalt put away iniquity far from thy tabernacles. Then shalt thou lay up gold as dust, and the gold of Ophir as the stones of the brooks. Yea, the Almighty shall be thy defence, and thou shalt have plenty of silver.
>
> Job 22:23-25

The word *defence* in this verse means "gold." In other words, God will be your Gold. God will be your Source. Now, we know that we don't look at God just as if He's a heavenly ATM. We know He is far more than that to us. He's our Father, our Healer, our Protector, our Guide, Savior, and Master—but He's also our Provider. So we could read those verses from Job this way: "Yeah, the Almighty will be your Gold, so then you'll lay up gold as dust, and the gold of Ophir as the stones of the brooks, and you'll have plenty of silver because the Almighty is your Gold; because the Almighty is your Source, because the Almighty is your Bank or your Banker, you'll have these results" (v. 24, paraphrased).

Psalm 37 says, "I have been young, and now am old; yet have I not seen the righteous forsaken, nor his seed begging bread" (v. 25). Why? Because the Lord is a Provider—and He provides with His riches in glory. There are many other verses that attest to the same truth about God. Proverbs chapter 8 talks about the wisdom of God, how it will cause you to inherit substance and will fill your treasures because God is the Bank. He's the Banker. Psalm 112 says, "If you fear God and delight greatly in His commandments, then wealth and riches will be in your house and your righteousness" (vv. 1-3, paraphrased). Some people have a problem with that. Wealth and riches and righteousness in the same Scripture? That's right. The verse goes on to promise, "It shall remain forever." Why? Because you fear God—because God is your Bank, God is your Source.

We must make a conscious decision to remember this during times like these when we are being inundated with bad financial news. It's nearly impossible to avoid it, so you must make a decision, and stick to it, that your source is not Wall Street, not Washington, not the government, not your job—but God. If someone took your job or sold your IRA out from under you, that doesn't mean anything. Your Source is the One who called Himself your "exceeding great reward." The One who called Himself your "gold" or your "defense." He is the One who called Himself Jehovah Jireh, El Shaddai. That is who your Source is. You've got to get your mind off what's going on in this world and instead meditate on the truth in God's Word. Let faith, not fear, rise up in your heart. Focus on God, not on what the media are telling you to focus on. Meditate on the fact that there is no recession in heaven and that God has promised you that His riches in glory are not impacted by those things. Find the Scriptures that say God is going to meet all your needs and take care of you during this time. Write them down. Memorize them. Proclaim them.

I'm a sports fan, and I don't get upset when the other team starts losing games. When the Chicago Bulls are having a bad season and it looks like they're in trouble, I don't get upset about it. If it looks like they're not going to make the playoffs, I don't care. Why? Because I'm a Detroit Pistons fan. All I care about is, Are the Pistons winning? The Bulls can lose, and I don't care because they're the other team. I'm only paying attention to my team.

That's the kind of focus we've got to have. No matter what's happening around us, it doesn't pertain to us. Pray for the people who are being hurt, and look for opportunities to bless them, but do not be concerned or afraid that you, too, will be hurt—because God is your Source according to His riches in glory. I'm not saying we shouldn't care about what's happening to other people. I am saying we should not look at what's happening to the other team and then be afraid for our own financial lives—because we are on a different team. We have a different Provider. We bank at a different bank.

As I'm writing this book, a number of banks are going out of business. People who banked there have been fearful about the money those banks have held for them. You may have banked at one of these banks—but let me remind you that God is your Source. Just because the world's financial system fails doesn't mean yours will.

Let's look at a psalm that is familiar to us. Psalm 23 begins with these comforting words: "The Lord is my shepherd" (v. 1). Notice it does not say Wall Street is my shepherd, or Coca-Cola, or whatever company for which you work. It doesn't say your 401(k) or your 403(b) is your shepherd. The Lord is your Shepherd. He is your Provider.

"I shall not want" (v. 1). There's nothing conditional about that verse. It is a statement that does not have an asterisk by it saying, "I shall not want except during a time of famine." It does not say, "God is going to be able to take care of me and my family unless . . ." There is no "unless" here. Nor is there an "except." It doesn't say, "Except for a time of famine or a recession or a real estate downturn."

"He maketh me to lie down in green pastures: he leadeth me beside the still waters" (v. 2). There is no "unless" here, either. If there's nothing around but brown pastures, rest assured that God will turn something that is brown to green for you. He has always set up *provision* for His people because He has *prevision;* He knows when things are coming, and He will set it up.

A minister told me recently that he allowed a friend to ride his motorcycle, not knowing that the man did not have the kind of experience necessary to ride that type of vehicle. The man attempted to make a turn, but because he didn't know what he was doing, he never made the turn. Instead, he kept going forward and went right off a cliff. This minister looked over the side of the cliff, and there was nothing but rocks. Way off in the distance, however, was one little patch of green. Guess where his friend landed? Not on the rocks that were all around him, but on that tiny patch of green. By that night, he was healed from the effects of the accident.

I'm here to tell you, it may be rocky all around you, and everybody else may be hitting the rocks, but God has got a green patch for you. He has an area where you'll have no lack, where indeed you'll see increase, where you'll eat of the fruit of the trees in that land, because God is a Shepherd who will make sure you do not lack.

"Thou preparest a table before me in the presence of mine enemies" (v. 5). Did you notice that there is not a Scripture where God says the enemies will have a table before you. No, it's always the other way around. He will prepare a table before you, in the presence of your enemies. In other words, you're going to have things on your table that will cause your enemies to be envious of you. Rest assured, those in the world will be envious of you, too, as they see you continue to increase while they decrease. That's part of why there are persecutions right now against Christians, preachers, and ministries; those in the world don't like to see you increase while they're struggling. I'm here to tell you, there's not a thing they can do about it. They can try whatever they want, but they cannot stop the Bank of Heaven from causing you to withdraw what you need, when you need it, and an abundance besides.

 God is your Source. God is your Banker. God is providing for you according to His great riches in glory.

"Thou preparest a table before me in the presence of mine enemies: thou anointest my head with oil; my cup runneth over. Surely goodness and mercy shall follow me all the days of my life: and I will dwell in the house of the Lord for ever" (vv. 5-6). Another word for *runneth over* is *overflows*. The word *goodness* is also translated *wealth* in Scripture. Goodness and mercy will follow you all the days of your life—not all the days except for the 2009 recession, not all the days except for when you made a dumb financial mistake. No, the Scripture says "all the days"—and that means every day, twenty-four/seven, 365 days a year. All the days of your life, money is chasing you down. Money is looking for you. Money is coming to your possession. God is increasing you more and more and more and more and more all the days of your life. Why? Because God is your Source. God is your Banker. God is providing for you according to His great riches in glory.

So what are you worried about? No wonder Jesus said, "Don't think about what you're going to drink or what you're going to wear or what you're going to eat. Don't worry about those things. I take care of the lilies. I take care of the birds. You're much greater than those things. You seek first the kingdom of God, and I'll make sure all these things are added to you. And I'll do it according to My great riches in glory."

Remember, the theme of this week's study is God's riches in glory and how God makes provision for us to tap into that. In 2 Corinthians chapter 9, Paul encourages the church to give to a specific offering. One of the reasons is because there was a kind of famine or lack in Jerusalem. Paul is encouraging the church at Corinth to give to the believers in Jerusalem so they would have no lack, even though the rest of the world around them did. Paul further tells what God would do for those who are cheerful and bountiful givers: "And God is able to make all grace abound toward you" (v. 8). Remember whom Paul is talking about here. It is God the Almighty, El Shaddai. He is able. He has the ability, the might, the wherewithal to make all grace abound. That is according to His riches in glory.

In the New Testament, sometimes the word *grace* refers to "the anointing to prosper," or we simply call it the blessing. There is something about the grace of God, the blessing, that will produce a manifestation on your behalf. Think about that. Heb. 4:16 says, "Let us therefore come boldly unto the throne of grace, that we may obtain mercy, and find grace to help in time of need." So that grace is going to bring about some actual help in time of need. That is similar to Mal. 3:10: "He will pour you out a blessing." He'll make it abound toward you. He'll make it bounce toward you. The blessing is coming toward you. It's being poured out on you. That's good news!

Why would He do that? What will the blessing do? The rest of 2 Cor. 9:8 gives the reason why God will give it to you: "That ye, always having all sufficiency in all things, may abound to every good work." There's that word again—*always*. Always would include any time of economic destruction, wouldn't it? Any time of economic downturn, right? *Always* means "all the time," doesn't it? So God is saying He is going to pour out His blessing on you, and He's going to give you access to His riches so that all the time you may abound and always you may have a sufficient portion. That means whether the stock market is at 13,000 or 8,000. All the time. If gas prices are $4 a gallon or $1 a gallon. "Always having all sufficiency." That means never lacking, never saying, "I don't have the money to pay for my mortgage this month." That means never being in a position where you can't pay your car note. That means never being in a position where you can't give as God wants you to give—like it's in your heart to give. That means "always having all sufficiency."

The word *sufficiency* means "self-satisfaction or contentment." When we talk about sufficiency, we think it means "enough," so we look at this Scripture and say, "That means that God is saying He'll just make sure you always have all that you need." Let's think about the word *enough*. When do you have enough food? When you're full. Many times I've gone to eat at my grandmother's house, and she made some of the best food in the world. We'll eat and eat and eat, and when I'm full, she'll say, "Have you had enough, baby?" Having enough is not just having enough to survive. When you go to the store, you don't buy just enough food so that you can make sure you live through tomorrow. That's not what God is talking about here. This word means "self-satisfaction or contentment." It's talking about being full, and that's what you see when you look at verse 11: "Being enriched in every thing to all bountifulness, which causeth through us thanksgiving to God." God is saying, "You'll be enriched in everything, and you'll be satisfied and content."

Verses 9 and 10 are in parentheses, so really what God says in verse 11 is just a different way of saying what He said in verse 8. He's talking about the same thing. He says He is going to put you in a position where He is able to cause you always to have enough so that you're satisfied in all things—in other words, in every area. Once again, verse 11 says, "Being enriched in every thing."

Are you beginning to see how God wants to enrich you in everything, always?

Day 11

SOME OIL, A FISH, AND A FAMINE

W E'RE CONTINUING OUR STUDY THIS WEEK OF GOD'S riches in glory. Today we're going to look at 1 Kings chapter 17, when there was a famine because of the wickedness of Jezebel. The prophet of God, Elijah, declared there would not be rain until he said it would rain. God told him to go to the brook Cherith, where ravens would feed him. True to God's Word, the ravens brought Elijah bread and flesh in the morning and in the evening, twice a day, and Elijah drank water from the brook.

Now, if the land was in the midst of a famine, most people were probably desperately looking for water and food, but God provided both for Elijah. When the brook dried up, God told him there was a widow in Zarephath whom He commanded to provide food for Elijah. The prophet traveled to her house, and as soon as he saw her, he said, "Give me a little water." She ran to do that, and then he said, "Give me a little cake, too."

She replied, "I don't have enough for my son and me to live on. In fact, we're about to have our last meal. My cupboards are bare. All I've got is a little bit of oil. We're going to eat what we have and then die."

God spoke to Elijah, and he said to her, "Look, if you'll go ahead and sow what you have now, God will make sure you don't run out throughout this famine." That's exactly what she did. She made a meal out of her last drops of food and gave it to the man of God. And God did a miracle and multiplied the food so that she and her household and Elijah ate for many days.

We often think of God's miracles as taking one object and another object, putting them together, and getting something new, but sometimes God doesn't even bother to do that. In this case, He just took the oil and reproduced it. He created more oil in the oil. It's similar to the miracle in 2 Kings chapter 4, where a widow was so in debt that she was about to lose her son. She told the prophet Elisha, "All I have is a pot of oil," and he said, "Take that oil, borrow some vessels, and pour the oil into it." God reproduced the oil in her house in such quantities that she was able to set up an oil business. It was oil from heaven. The man of God told her, "Now take that oil, sell it, pay off all your debts, and live off the rest." That would be as if you took all the money you have in the bank, piled it up on your living room floor, and watched God reproduce it over and over and over until the bills were stacked all the way to the ceiling.

There's another miracle of multiplication in John chapter 6. A crowd of at least 5,000 people followed Jesus to hear Him speak, and the only food to feed them was five loaves and two fishes. How did

God take care of His people? Jesus took the food and blessed it, and they started passing it around. All of a sudden, the food started multiplying. God didn't have to add anything to make that happen. The only added ingredient was the blessing. Once He added the blessing, that bread and fish had to multiply. They couldn't do anything but multiply.

> He can do abundantly above what you can think. In fact, He can do "exceeding abundantly above" what you can think.

I'm here to tell you that once He puts the blessing on your financial life, you get what verse 10 talks about: God multiplies the seed you have sown. He multiplies what belongs to you. God causes you to increase more and more and more. That's what He did before, and He's the same God today that He was then. If He did it in famine then, He'll do it in famine now. And if He'll do it in famine now, He'll do it in famine in the days to come. That's why you can boldly declare, "He always provides for me because He is more than able to do it according to His riches in glory—always."

Think about it. He can do not just above what you can think. He can do abundantly above what you can think. In fact, He can do "exceeding abundantly above" what you can think. In other words, you can't even begin to think about what God can do. You can't even fathom what He can actually do. So don't let the enemy try to tell you God can't do something that you *can* fathom. I don't know about you, but I can imagine having no debts. I can imagine being a millionaire with a mission. I can imagine being a billionaire who goes around to churches and pays off their building drives church after church after church, so that they can preach the gospel. I can imagine that.

So if I can think it, then God can do it—"exceeding abundantly above" it. And if He can do that, then I know He can take care of me—in the middle of what the world is calling a recession. We're talking about the God who put a coin at the bottom of the sea and had a fish go after it so that Jesus' and Peter's taxes could be paid for. The fish went to the bottom, grabbed the money, got up, and jumped on a hook.

This is the same God who had a great fish swallow a man and spit him out three days later. God stopped the sun in the middle of a battle because one of his men asked him to. Another time God sped it up a little bit. Science proves that. God took a Man who had been crucified on a cross and was in hell for three days, and brought Him out victoriously—and He changed the world. What's a little money to Him? It's nothing. The Bank of Heaven is unlimited. That's why you should let God be your Banker. He's never going to turn down your loan. You don't have to worry about bank fees. You don't have to worry about a note because in His system, there's no credit involved; it's cash. (We'll cover that more in a couple of weeks.)

You don't fear because God is your Source if you bank at the Bank of Jehovah. God always makes sure your needs are taken care of. If you'll step into God's system, you're going to see increase during this time. Don't put your faith on the shelf and say, "I guess God can't do it now." No, this is the time you keep thanking God and believing Him—in spite of what you may see personally as well as what you may see in the world.

I had to read my own book, *God is Making You Rich,* about a month ago. God had me pick it up again "just because"—just to keep fighting the fight of faith. That's what you need to do, too: Just keep on fighting, keep on believing, keep on fighting, keep on believing. Keep ignoring what you're seeing, and believe God like you did when you were first saved. That's what you want to do. You want to make sure that you just keep believing God, that you learn from Abraham and pay no attention to the circumstances. Keep giving God glory and praise for your victory, and it will come. It will come to pass.

Take it from somebody who is sitting on the other side of that battle. I've come through the valley. I've preached about going through the valley. I've come through the valley, and it looked dark. There was a long season when I wondered, *Does light even exist?* But you keep believing God, and God will bring you through it. God is not taking a vacation because the news media say there's a recession. If anything, He's working overtime making sure His people are getting into His system so they can really see the financial results He wants them to see.

Day 12

A God of Prevision
Who Has Provision

L ET'S BEGIN TODAY BY LOOKING AT THE LIFE OF JOSEPH IN
Genesis chapter 45. Joseph was a young man who had a dream
that he was going to rule over his family. He, unfortunately,
shared his dream with his brothers and soon found himself sold into
slavery by his brother when he was about seventeen. Joseph became
a slave in the house of Potiphar, but God's blessing operating in his
life caused him to increase until he became second in command. A
woman lied about him, saying he had raped her, and he ended up in
prison—but the blessing was on him. He ended up being second in
command in prison.

When Pharaoh had a dream, because of the anointing on Joseph and the favor of God, he was able to give Pharaoh the interpretation of that dream. Joseph once again became second in command—this time of all of Egypt. He was only thirty years old. The blessing was not exhausted yet. (Remember, it is exceeding abundantly above what we can imagine.) God told Joseph that there were going to be seven years of plenty and then seven years of famine, so Joseph helped Egypt prepare. During the seven good years, they saved crops and money and stored them in preparation. Sure enough, famine arrived—along with Joseph's brothers. They had run out of money and heard a rumor that Egypt had plenty. Two years after they arrived, Joseph finally revealed to them that he was their brother— and in so doing, he said something about God's plan for his life.

> And Joseph said unto his brethren, Come near to me, I pray you. And they came near. And he said, I am Joseph your brother, whom ye sold into Egypt. Now therefore be not grieved, nor angry with yourselves, that ye sold me hither: for God did send me before you to preserve life. For these two years hath the famine been in the land: and yet there are five years, in the which there shall neither be earing nor harvest. And God sent me before you to preserve you a posterity in the earth, and to save your lives by a great deliverance.
>
> Gen. 45:4-7

The word *posterity* means a portion. God sent Joseph ahead of his brothers to make sure there was a portion for them in the earth. "He sent me to save your life," Joseph told them. Remember, there were promises associated with this family line, and if Jacob and his family all died in the famine, God's future kingdom, Israel, would be in peril. If God didn't do something, there would be no Israel. So God took a young man by the name of Joseph, who was faithful to Him, and provided for him in exceedingly abundant ways. I don't believe that God wanted Joseph's brothers to sell him into slavery, but the bottom line is that God got him to Egypt and had this young man go through on-the-job training. You don't just walk in and become prime minister of Egypt and do well when you've never run anything before. So Joseph ran Potiphar's house, he ran the prison, and finally, he ran Egypt. Jacob and his family may or may not have been doing what they were supposed to; we know his brothers obviously were wicked once upon a time. But God had Joseph go through all that training and preparation so that when the famine hit, there would be provision already prepared for them. God looked ahead twenty-two years. He used Joseph to prepare for the years of famine so that Israel would be provided for, to save their lives. God is a God of prevision, so He has provision.

 Like Joseph, you just need to be where God told you to be and do what God told you to do, and you'll find that the provision has been waiting for you.

Now let's move to today. Way back in history, God was able to look at 2009 and your financial life and see that there was going to be a financial collapse. He could see that people were going to be losing their jobs and their savings, and that there would be great panic. He could see all these negative things happening, and He could see that unless He provided for His people—unless He provided for you— you would be impacted. But God prepared a Joseph for you. Let me repeat that: God has got a Joseph for you. It may be a job; it may be a God idea that is producing income and wealth for you; it may be a business that He's giving you; it may be somebody whom God's just going to send across your path to be a blessing to you individually.

I'm here to tell you, God was not surprised when the stock market crashed. God was not surprised when Wall Street fell apart. God was not surprised when whatever happened to you happened to you. God was not shocked. God has prevision. He has already made provision for you. It's already there. You don't need to be worried or concerned. Like Joseph, you just need to be where God told you to be and do what God told you to do, and you'll find that the provision has been waiting for you. God has preserved posterity for you to save your financial life in the midst of destruction, to give you great deliverance, and to show the world that He is the almighty God, the King of all Kings, and the Lord of all Lords. He has already made a way. He's the God who makes a way in the wilderness and a river in the desert.

He's already done it. He already worked it out, and He already provided it. You need to open up your eyes and say, "Lord, I understand you're my Source." You need to lift your hand and say, "Lord, I thank You for it in advance." You need to run, shout, dance, and believe in God that it is so—and then watch it come to pass. He's already made a way. He's already put it on layaway, and it's been there all this time. Now it's time for a withdrawal. It's like a parent who laid up money for his or her child so that when the child turned old enough, there would be funds sitting there for college. God has been saving up for you. It's time now to withdraw.

Do you need more examples? How about how God fed Israel for forty years in the wilderness? Remember, they came out of Egypt, and there was no water. When they reached Marah, the water was bitter. God said, "Throw the tree in the water." Now, isn't that amazing? In the middle of a wilderness, there is some water and there is a tree. God turned the water into sweet water, and they refreshed themselves with it. Then they kept walking and found a place called Elim with twelve wells of water—in the desert! Can you see how God already provided for them in that wilderness? It was already there. They just had to keep following God.

How about Isaac? He was in a time of famine and was thinking about going down to Egypt, but God said, "No, you stay here. I'll put my blessing on you here. I'll prosper you here." God did exactly what He said; He put His blessing on him, prospered him, and in the midst of famine when the ground doesn't produce—that's why it's famine—Isaac sowed seed and gave a hundredfold. God took that and began to bless Isaac. He continued to increase and got richer and richer and richer and richer, to a point where the Bible says he was so rich that the king said, "Leave us." Even when they needed water in a time of famine, his men dug a well and found water there—in famine. You just don't do that in a famine!

When they found water, of course the Philistines got upset. "No, no, that's our water," they said. Being the man of God, Isaac said, "You know what? Take it. Let's go over here and dig." What happened? They found more water already there waiting for them.

The Philistines said, "No, no, no, that's our water, too," but Isaac said, "Fine, take it." He moved on, dug another well, and guess what he found? More water. He called it Rehoboth and said, "The Lord has made room for us."

God has made room for you, too. You've just got some digging to do. You've just got to find out what God wants you to do, and you need to get to work on what your assignment is. It goes back to Matt. 6:33, which directs us, "Seek ye first the kingdom of God." Helping God grow His kingdom on earth means doing things His way. And that means doing what God has called you to do, doesn't it? That's part of it. Whatever God has called you to do helps the kingdom. So let's not be focused on the economy. Let's go back to being focused on our assignment. Let's go back to being focused on doing things God's way. Let's not stop doing things God's way because the world's financial system is failing. Let's not stop blessing others, particularly charities that always suffer when there is financial trouble because people stop giving. Christians should not cut back on giving when things get tough. We're going to study that more later in our challenge. But I want to mention it here so that you see the connection; if God is your Source according to His riches in glory, why would you even need to think about cutting back on your giving? Your Source is God, not the economy. Our giving creates deposits into the Bank of Heaven. It's because we deposit that we're able to withdraw. If we stop depositing, then all of a sudden, we can't withdraw.

Did you know that you can create your own recession? And it doesn't have anything to do with the Bank of Heaven running out of funds. We've seen through the lives of Joseph, Isaac, and others that the Bank of Heaven has limitless supplies and resources—according to God's riches in glory. So if you create your own recession, it's not because God is running out of money. It is because you stopped doing things His way. My giving hasn't changed one bit, even while I've been believing God for some things. If anything, I will give more because I'm seeking first the kingdom of God. I keep doing things God's way, even with my finances. And now I can withdraw from the Bank of Heaven. Now I can receive those blessings that God has for me and those around me. I'll come across that place called Elim and find the well that God already provided for me. I'll be able to say, "The Lord has made room for me." That is why I can boldly declare, "Not in my house! There's no recession here!"

Day 13

GROUP DISCUSSION

Action point: Have faith in God.

Action Scripture: "So then faith cometh by hearing, and hearing by the word of God" (Rom. 10:17).

Action step: Read through finance Scriptures found in the appendix this week to build your faith. Highlight the ones that seem to jump out at you.

Questions:

1. What did you read in our study this week that surprised you? That caused you to change how you thought about God and His ways? That motivated you to continue on the twenty-eight-day challenge?

2. Why can God provide for you in a recession? Which of the examples you read this week have encouraged you that He can?

3. Share a time when you were in great need and God supernaturally provided for you. How did you see His *prevision* supply your *provision*?

4. Name a Bible story when God provided for one of His servants during famine. Is it possible that God has already arranged to provide for you during this time of your life?

5. This week we read a Scripture with the word "always" in it. Do you remember what it was? How have you seen that come to pass in your own life? How does God promise you it will come to pass in the future? How do you need to change your thinking and your speaking to align with that?

6. Which financial Scriptures did you highlight from the appendix? Share why they were particularly meaningful to you.

Day 14

REST

To think about today: At group discussion this week, you shared about the financial Scriptures in the appendix that seemed particularly meaningful to you. Today, choose one of them and meditate on it throughout the day. You may want to write out the verse on a card so you can carry it with you. Allow the Lord to speak to you through His Word while you go about your activities of the day.

Week 3

SWITCHING BANKS

Day 15

A TALE OF TWO BANKS

THIS WEEK OUR FOCUS IS ON FINDING OUT WHERE YOU'VE been banking and who your banker is, determining if you need to switch banks, and then studying how to make the switch so that Jesus is your Banker.

You already know I've made a decision not to participate in the recession. I've chosen to sit this one out. In fact, I've decided to sit them all out until the Lord returns. Would you like to experience that? Would you like to not be concerned about losing your house, your car, your job, or your savings? Would you like to get to the point that you actually expect to increase—even while others are experiencing decrease?

You certainly can. You can begin by asking yourself two important questions: Where is my bank? Who is my banker? If your city is anything like Atlanta, there is a bank on every corner. In reality, however, there are only two banks: the Bank of the World and the Bank of Heaven. Most Christians will say, "Oh, yeah, I'm banking at the Bank of Heaven. I'm on heaven's side," but it's one thing to say it, and another to do it.

Think about how you use a bank. You use it to deposit money and then to withdraw money when you need it, or take out a loan if you don't have the money. When you want to buy a home, you go get money from the bank, and the bank finances your home. When you want to get a vehicle, you use the bank to finance that vehicle. If you want to start a business, you go to the bank and get a business loan. All those transactions take place in both the Bank of the World and the Bank of Heaven—but how they take place is completely different.

Let's begin by looking at some of the characteristics of the Bank of the World. To understand how it operates, we can study Genesis chapter 11, which paints a perfect picture of what is commonly called the Babylonian system in the earth—that is, the world's system. It's the world attempting to meet the needs of man without God. This is really the first time we see it in Scripture:

> And the whole earth was of one language, and of one speech. And it came to pass, as they journeyed from the east, that they found a plain in the land of Shinar; and they dwelt there. And they said one to another, Go to, let us make brick, and burn them thoroughly. And they had brick for stone, and slime had they for morter. And they said, Go to, let us build us a city and a tower, whose top may reach unto heaven; and let us make us a name, lest we be scattered abroad upon the face of the whole earth.
>
> Gen. 11:1-4

Remember, this takes place not long after the flood. This was the whole earth at that time. They said, "Let us build a tower and a city.

Let us make a name." When we talk about that passage, we often refer to just the tower, but they were after much more than a tower. They were after a city and making a name for themselves. The word *name* implies "a memorial of greatness, an honor." Who is not mentioned there? God. In other words, they were saying, "Let us build a great civilization without God."

Here is the epitome of the Babylonian system: attempting to meet the needs and, ultimately, desires of man without God. Did they know of God? Yes. They were not that far removed from God's causing the flood to wipe almost all of mankind off the face of the earth. They knew Him, but they elected to push Him out and do it on their own. They believed together, "We can without God."

> And the Lord came down to see the city and the tower, which the children of men builded. And the Lord said, Behold, the people is one, and they have all one language; and this they begin to do: and now nothing will be restrained from them, which they have imagined to do. Go to, let us go down, and there confound their language, that they may not understand one another's speech. So the Lord scattered them abroad from thence upon the face of all the earth: and they left off to build the city. Therefore is the name of it called Babel; because the Lord did there confound the language of all the earth: and from thence did the Lord scatter them abroad upon the face of all the earth.
>
> Vv. 5-9

The Bible says in Prov. 10:22, "The blessing of the Lord, it maketh rich, and he addeth no sorrow with it." What is this referring to, and why did God find the need to say this? Because making money according to the Babylonian system means you are going to have sorrow. God told Adam in the Garden of Eden after his sin, "In the sweat of thy face shalt thou eat bread" (Gen. 3:19). In other words, it is going to be difficult for you now. It's going to bring fatigue and grief. To bring forth the provision that you need, from now on, you'll have to do it on your own—without Me. It is going to be far more difficult.

When the nation of Israel was in Egypt, they were slaves made to work hard labor. They didn't even have the tools and resources to do what was required of them. It was very difficult labor. This is what a lot of people are experiencing in the twenty-first century. They can hardly stand to get up in the morning to even go to work because it is so difficult and because they hate it so much. Even those who do love their work find they're still doing it with toil—either because it requires so much of their time that it causes an imbalance in their life, or because they're just not making enough money for all the hours they put in. Imagine a woman or a man who becomes a partner at a law firm. Now he or she is working seventy hours a week, and what happens? There's so much stress on the person's home life that he or she ends up getting a divorce. The person loses his or her kids. He or she doesn't even have that many friends anymore, and this person has been alienated from his or her family. That job cost that person so much because of toil. God doesn't want us to toil anymore, but if you operate according to the Babylonian system, you are going to take care of yourself without God. You are going to work hard, and it is going to be difficult. And you just might not be able to provide for yourself, anyway.

Work without partnering with God the Father is difficult and will lead you nowhere. It's like kids. Picture an eight-year-old boy and his little brother as they try to build a tree house by themselves. You know they're not going to be able to pull that off on their own. Eventually, they're going to need some help. If they try to do it without their dad's help, it's not going to have success; they'll never get off the ground. But if they ask for his help, that tree house will get built.

It seems right to some people to do things without God. That's banking at the Bank of the World.

My little daughters are very independent. I thought it was just my first one. Whenever I tried to help her with a homework assignment, she'd say, "I don't need your help!" Now my second daughter has started saying the same thing: "I don't need your help!" A minute or two later, I'd hear, "Daddy, I need help!" We've all heard about older kids who are so upset with their parents and their rules that they declare, "I don't need you. I'm going to run away and take care of myself." What happens? They come crawling back home, saying, "I'm so sorry. I do need you. Things are a lot harder out there than I thought they were. I'll do what you say."

The Bible says, "There is a way which seemeth right unto a man, but the end thereof are the ways of death" (Prov. 14:12). It seems right to some people to do things without God. That's banking at the Bank of the World. If you decide to do things according to the Babylonian system, you are going to attempt it without God. The end result is going to be lack in some area. *I will do whatever job I want. I'll use whatever values I have.* Often that means cheating, stealing, and doing whatever it takes. God's way surely isn't doing it without God.

In Genesis chapter 12, God told Abraham, "Leave the country you're in. Come to My land" (v. 1, paraphrased). What was God doing? He was causing Abraham to switch from one bank to another. Abraham responded and moved where God told him to, and as a result, God blessed him abundantly and prospered him. Yet what happened when a famine came? Abraham went back to the old system. Instead of relying on God as his Provider and Banker, he went down to Egypt and made a mess of things. In the Bible, Egypt typically represents man's system of provision. It also is a type of a kingdom of darkness.

Abraham had a beautiful wife, Sarah, and he was so afraid the Egyptians were going to kill him because of his wife that he lied and said she was his sister. Notice he wasn't afraid of that when he was following God; when you get out from under God's protection, all of a sudden, you are in danger. Pharaoh took his wife, Sarah, thinking she was Abraham's sister, but God was merciful and put a plague on the house of Pharaoh. Pharaoh figured out where that was coming from. He told Abraham, "This is your wife, not your sister!" and he kicked Abraham and his entire family out of Egypt, sending them off with money and provision.

Abraham left Egypt a very rich man—but he didn't get it God's way, so it brought negative results. Years later his son was in the same situation, and years beyond that, so was the entire nation of Israel. Satan does that. He will bring the same attack, the same temptation, to different generations. That is how generational curses come to a family and keep on working.

In Genesis chapter 26, it all repeats. "And there was a famine in the land, beside the first famine that was in the days of Abraham. And Isaac went unto Abimelech king of the Philistines unto Gerar" (v. 1). Isaac went to Abimelech because his father had a covenant with him, which meant Isaac would have favor with him. Abimelech was someone who would be willing to help him. Isaac lacked provision because famine had sapped his resources, and he knew Abimelech had some good resources. This was a pretty big famine; it was beyond recession. It was a depression. So Isaac went to Abimelech seeking provision. He was actively seeking provision—and he went to Abimelech, not to God, to find it. We might say he switched from the Bank of Heaven to the Bank of the World.

I can hear Isaac now. "You know those people in Egypt. They built themselves a city and a tower. That's a little stronger than what they have over here in Gerar, so I'm going to head down to Egypt, and maybe they can help me and give me some provision."

The Lord, however, wasn't about to let that happen. "And the Lord appeared unto him and said, 'Go not down to Egypt'" (v. 2). This isn't a suggestion. It is a command. To disobey that is to sin. "Don't you go back into that." In other words, "Don't go back to that system." Isaac had been living on a level where God was his Source, and he was about to go back to the world being his source. Instead, he sowed in the land God gave him, and the blessing was on him, which caused him to receive back a hundredfold. Isaac became richer and richer. All that happened because he did not go back to that Babylonian system. He stayed in the kingdom system. He didn't bank at the Bank of the World. He banked at the Bank of Heaven.

Many generations later, the children of Israel were in Egypt as slaves, where they were held in bondage to the world's system. God brought them out and let them be in the wilderness so they could understand they didn't live by bread alone, but by every word of God. God taught them, "When you are hooked up with Me and you're in a covenant with Me, you live by every word of Mine. If I say bread will fall from heaven, it will fall from heaven. If I say water will come from a rock, water will come from a rock. What I say is what will happen. Then you will have provision just because I said it, not because the world produced it." That is the Bank of Heaven versus the Bank of the World.

The Bible says in Psalm 127:1, "Except the Lord build the house, they labour in vain that build it." I encourage you to think about which bank you've been doing business at. I want you to be ready so that when the enemy comes to attack, you will be able to declare boldly, "Not in my house!"

Day 16

WHICH BANK IS YOUR BANK?

ARE YOU BEGINNING TO SEE THERE ARE CONSEQUENCES for doing business with the Bank of the World? Picture this scenario. You go to your bank where you've deposited your money for years. You want to withdraw enough for your rent, but when you get to the window, the teller says, "I'm sorry, but we don't have any money today."

"But this is my money," you reply. "I need it. If I don't have this money—my money—I'm going to be on the street."

"I'm sorry, we just don't have it."

That is the Bank of the World. Or imagine going to your bank and asking for a loan to buy a house. "Sure, we can help you buy a house," the loan officer says. "But you have to be a slave to us."

"What?" you gasp.

"You have to work so many years doing work for the bank, and after you do, the home will be yours."

"How many years are you talking about?"

"We'll let you know when the time comes."

That is the Bank of the World. This bank requires never-ending deposits, but withdrawals come with strings attached. You end up being a slave your entire life to the Bank of the World to pay for all the things you keep getting because unfortunately, most people don't stop at just a house. They get a car. They get furniture and then a big-screen TV and then the latest computer. They start getting clothes. They have five or six or ten credit cards. When you operate in that Babylonian system, it is a never-ending downward spiral.

The Bank of the World also will charge you interest. In Exodus chapter 22, God told His people not to take interest when they give a loan to a poor person. In Deuteronomy chapter 23, He told them not to take interest when they make a loan to a fellow believer. Ps. 15:5 highlights that one of the traits of a man of God is that he refuses to take interest when he sends out a loan. It causes God to say, "I'm going to bless him and increase him." You'll also find this in Exodus chapter 18 and Proverbs chapter 28. According to the Bible, usury (or excessive interest, according to some translations) is unjust gain. Would you agree there is some excessive interest in our country—and that it's a normal occurrence? Many companies and banks don't charge you simple interest; they compound it. That's a sign of the Bank of the World.

You, however, don't have to do business with the Bank of the World. There's another option. It's called the Bank of Heaven. To show you the difference between the two, let's imagine a twelve-year-old boy who has encountered a number of difficult things in his young life. When he was born, his father left his mother. Just before he turned twelve, his mother got strung out on drugs, and he ended up on his own. Now he's living on the streets, focused on finding food every day and a place to sleep at night. He's slipped through the system, which we know happens, and now he's focused on mere survival. His mission is to find provision and to survive.

That is what Jesus was referring to when He talked about those who are without God. They are seeking provision so they can survive. The Bible says they are bound by the fear of death. In Hebrews chapter 2, we learn that Jesus delivered us from that fear so we don't have to be afraid of death—either physical or spiritual—but those in the world, including this little boy, are driven by fear.

 The Bank of Heaven has your best interests in mind. It exists to prosper you and bless you so you, in turn, can be a blessing to others.

Now let's look at another twelve-year-old boy. This child lives with both his parents. They've provided a roof over his head, food on the table—as much as he wants. He has a bed. He's able to go to a good school that teaches him about God and helps him to get a good education. His focus isn't on provision. His focus is on education. He isn't interested in just surviving. He's actually interested in being a success.

Do you see the difference? This boy represents those who bank at the Bank of Heaven. That is how people who bank at the Bank of Heaven live. They don't have to be worried about where the next check is going to come from to pay the rent or the car note.

They're not focused on that; instead, they're focused on helping God accomplish His purpose.

The Bank of Heaven has your best interests in mind. It exists to prosper you and bless you so you, in turn, can be a blessing to others. In Luke chapter 5, Jesus introduced Peter to this bank. Peter had been out all night fishing and had caught nothing. That was their livelihood and their business. Jesus told him, "Launch your boat into the deep for a draught." And Peter said, "We've already been out there. We've been fishing all day. We didn't catch anything." That's the Bank of the World. Peter couldn't make any withdrawals, but Jesus was about to introduce him to a new bank. At first Peter complained, as we all do, saying, "I tried that already," but at the Lord's urging, he tried it again. The result? The Bank of Heaven brought in a great harvest for him.

Jesus said, "Seek ye first the kingdom of God" (Matt. 6:33). Another way to put it is, "Focus your attention on the kingdom of God." If you are seeking—or focusing on—all your needs, you're not seeking first the kingdom. Your needs have your focus, and that's what you're seeking. If you do business at the Bank of the World, your needs will never be properly met, so of course you'll constantly need to focus on them. That's one of Satan's ploys. If he can get your attention off God and what He wants you to do, and keep it on meeting your needs and stressing over where the money will come from for your next mortgage payment, he's accomplished his goal.

When you do business with the Bank of Heaven, however, this is what God promises you: "Seek ye first the kingdom of God . . . *and all these things shall be added unto you*" (emphasis added). That promise means if you seek God first, He'll take care of the rest. So when Jesus says, "Seek ye first the kingdom of God," what should your response be? You should say, "If God wants me witnessing to people, I'm going to witness to people. If God wants me praying for people, giving to people, encouraging people, or discipling people, I'm going to do it. If God wants me serving people, whether it is in the church or in the community, I am going to do it. That is my number one priority, not just trying to put food on the table, a roof over my head, and clothes on my back, because I know the Bank of Heaven is taking care of all those things. I can just focus on my education. I can focus on success in God. I can focus on helping God expand His kingdom, knowing all these other things will be added unto me."

Jesus is saying to you, "Focus on your mission." When you bank at the Bank of Heaven, you can focus on your mission because you are seeking first the kingdom of God, not your own kingdom. You're seeking His righteousness, which the Amplified Bible says is "His way of doing and being right." Remember that Matt. 6:33 was written before Jesus died and rose again. We automatically think, "I've got a right standing with God because I have received Jesus into my life." That is completely accurate, of course, but He wasn't talking about that kind of righteousness because He hadn't died yet at this point. He wasn't talking about the righteousness you receive by faith, the righteousness you attain by doing right. When the Old Testament referred to the just, it meant those who lived their lives in a way that was consistent with God's Word—those who did things God's way. So we could paraphrase Jesus' words in Matt. 6:33 this way: "Your mission ought to be to do things My way, to operate like I operate, to be like Me. Your mission ought to be to become an individual who is doing right and therefore is right."

 If the Holy Spirit is stirring you and you know you've been doing business at the wrong bank, it's not too late to make a change. God's mercy is never-failing.

Ps. 34:9 says, "Fear the Lord, ye his saints: for there is no want to them that fear him. The young lions do lack, and suffer hunger: but they that seek the Lord shall not want any good thing." The youngest lions are the strongest of the pack. They're the leaders, the elite. They seem to have all the intelligence and connections, but they're operating in the world's system. They're banking at the wrong bank, so although they look like they have it all together, they still lack. Even if they have money, they lack in other areas. But those who fear the Lord—who seek Him—won't lack any good thing. He didn't just say they will have their needs met. He said they won't lack for any good thing. Ps. 84:11 says, "No good thing will he withhold from them that walk uprightly."

If the Holy Spirit is stirring you and you know you've been doing business at the wrong bank, it's not too late to make a change. God's mercy is never-failing, and He will partner with you to help you change banks. Prov. 10:22 describes what happens when you begin a relationship with the Bank of Heaven: "The blessing of the Lord, it maketh rich, and he addeth no sorrow with it." I want you to notice the blessing; it is God's empowerment to prosper, God's ability on your ability, heaven on earth in your life. A key word in this verse is the word *it,* which refers to the blessing of the Lord. It's not you who maketh rich; it's not the government that makes rich; it's the blessing of the Lord that maketh rich.

When you invest in the Bank of Heaven and decide to let Jesus be your Banker, God's blessing brings about your dreams. *It* maketh rich. There is no toil for you—no fatigue or grief. It is work without sweat. You've probably experienced this, particularly as a new Christian. When you get into what God has called you to do, it's easy for you. It's not that you don't have to be diligent, but it comes naturally to you because that is what you were born to do. You were wired for it. You were sent for that purpose. That is the blessing of God on your life.

So when you are banking at the Bank of Heaven, and as the blessing is doing the job of making you rich, what does that allow you to focus on? It allows you to focus on the kingdom of God (not on your needs). Remember: "Seek ye first the kingdom of God, and his righteousness; and all these things shall be added unto you" (Matt. 6:33). That means you are free to seek first the kingdom of God because you don't have to worry about where your next meal is coming from. You're free to hear God's voice and do whatever He tells you to do. In the process, you start blessing those around you instead of just thinking of your own well-being.

Remember what God promised Abraham? "Follow Me, go to my land, and I will bless you and make your name great. Then you will be a blessing" (Gen. 12:2, paraphrased). You not only get a blessing, but you become a blessing. In fact, you get the blessing by being a blessing. When the Bank of Heaven brings you finances, it does it first and foremost so that you can bless people. Jesus said it is more blessed to give than to receive.

A number of years ago, there was a movie called *Brewster's Millions,* starring Richard Pryor. He had to give away $3 million in a certain amount of time, and if he did, he would get $30 million. So he was looking for ways to get rid of the money. When you think about how God wants us to live, it's not all that different. We should be looking for ways to bless others. The more we do, the more blessings will come our way. Paul reminded us to help take care of the weak and that Jesus said, "It is more blessed to give than to receive" (Acts 20:35). When you operate according to the Bank of the World, you're consumed with receiving, but when you decide to switch banks, you are consumed with giving. You will want to be debt-free, not just so you can do what you want with your money, although, thank God, you will be able to do that, but because you'll be consumed with blessing others. Remember, God doesn't have a problem with your driving a nice car and living in a nice house, but that's not what you're living for. You are living to give. You're blessed to be a blessing.

Gal. 6:10 says, "As we have therefore opportunity, let us do good unto all men, especially unto them who are of the household of faith." That sounds to me like I ought to be on the lookout for opportunity. So if I let opportunity pass me by, I just disobeyed that Scripture because God said whenever an opportunity shows up, do good. That's the difference between doing things man's way and doing things God's way. If I'm looking for opportunity to give, then I get what Prov. 11:24 promises: "There is that scattereth, and yet increaseth; and there is that withholdeth more than is meet, but it tendeth to poverty."

Ps. 112 has a detailed description of the blessings experienced by the person who hears bad reports (let's say of impending recession), but refuses to budge from the Bank of Heaven:

> He shall not be afraid of evil tidings: his heart is fixed, trusting in the Lord. His heart is established, he shall not be afraid, until he see his desire upon his enemies. He hath dispersed, he hath given to the poor; his righteousness endureth for ever; his horn shall be exalted with honour. The wicked shall see it, and be grieved; he shall gnash with his teeth, and melt away: the desire of the wicked shall perish.
>
> Vv. 7-10

He has dispersed abroad. He is gracious. He gives to the poor. This is a man who gives and gives and gives. What happens? God exalts him with honor (and the wicked see it). What's more, his righteousness endureth forever. In other words, he not only gets harvest in this life, but he gets harvest in the next life.

That is what Jesus was talking about when He said, "Lay not up for yourselves treasures upon earth, where moth and rust doth corrupt, and where thieves break through and steal" (Matt. 6:19). Some people think He meant we shouldn't have any money here on earth. If that's what He meant, then He contradicted Himself in Luke 6:38 and many other places throughout the Bible. This is what He meant: Don't focus on getting treasures for yourself. Don't become the unjust man in Luke chapter 16 who got a great harvest and said, "Now what shall I do? I'm going to build greater barns, kick up my feet, and be at ease for the rest of my life."

God says, "You fool! You are going to lose your life tonight, and now who is going to enjoy what you have?" Don't live to get. Don't live to hoard. Don't lay up treasure for yourself. No, instead, lay up treasure in heaven—in the Bank of Heaven—because this produces fruit. You get treasure in heaven when you are a blessing to others on behalf of God, just like the man described in Psalm 112.

At some point, there is going to be a rapture. At some point, life as we know it on this planet is going to be different. You are going to be sitting in eternity, and whatever money you have in your pocket right now won't help you at all. The concrete in heaven is gold; how could that compare to the paper you have in your pocket? But when you bank at the Bank of Heaven, you lay up treasure that is going to last you for all of eternity. When you live your Christian life looking for opportunities to give, to bless, to show people the love of God, it will bring about financial increase in your life today and lay up treasure for you in heaven forever. We looked at Prov. 11:24 earlier; here it is again with the next verse:

> There is that scattereth, and yet increaseth; and there is that withholdeth more than is meet, but it tendeth to poverty. The liberal soul shall be made fat: and he that watereth shall be watered also himself.
>
> Vv. 24-25

Why are these Scriptures in the Bible? Did you ever think about that? Is the writer just telling us about somebody—or does he want you to be the one who is scattering? Notice that the person he describes scatters, and money keeps coming. Yet the wicked—the one banking at the Bank of the World—tries to hold on to his money, but he loses it. That's the Babylonian system. If you bank there, you can expect eventual ruin, but if you bank at the Bank of Heaven, you can scatter to your heart's content, and you're always going to get more.

Here are more benefits in this verse: "The liberal soul shall be made fat" (v. 25). The liberal person is the one who scatters, who is a consistently generous giver. What does he get in return? He is made financially fat. The Amplified Bible says he'll be enriched. He waters, and he himself is watered.

2 Cor. 9:8 says, " And God is able to make all grace abound toward you; that ye, always having all sufficiency in all things, may abound to every good work." I want you to notice the phrase "always having all sufficiency in all things." Here's how the Amplified Bible says it:

> And God is able to make all grace (every favor and earthly blessing) come to you in abundance, so that you may always and under all circumstances and whatever the need be self-sufficient [possessing enough to require no aid or support and furnished in abundance for every good work and charitable donation].

That sounds to me like being debt-free, and we're going to look at that on a future day in this challenge. For now, I want you to see that being debt-free is one of the benefits of banking at the Bank of Heaven. It doesn't happen automatically, and there are things you have to do to cooperate with God, but this Scripture promises that God can get you to a place where you are self-sufficient and debt-free. When you are, you'll have an abundance for others. Can you see the benefit?

Thus you will be enriched in all things and in every way, so that you can be generous, and [your generosity as it is] administered by us will bring forth thanksgiving to God. For the service that the ministering of this fund renders does not only fully supply what is lacking to the saints (God's people), but it also overflows in many [cries of] thanksgiving to God. Because at [your] standing of the test of this ministry, they will glorify God for your loyalty and obedience to the Gospel of Christ which you confess, as well as for your generous-hearted liberality to them and to all [the other needy ones].

Vv. 11-13 AMP

There are three benefits in this one passage: You are blessed, you are able to be a blessing to others, and God gets all the glory. Who wouldn't want to do business with a bank that gives such great returns on your investment?

FIVE SIGNS YOU'RE
BANKING AT THE
WRONG PLACE

I'M A BIG FAN OF SCIENCE FICTION, INCLUDING A TV SHOW called "Battlestar Galactica." I'm not saying it's the greatest show in the world, but I enjoy it. The story line features two groups of characters: humans and the Cylons. On the new "Battlestar Galactica," the Cylons can look like humans, so occasionally, one will realize it is really a Cylon and that its entire life, it has been a Cylon and didn't know it.

You may have spent your entire life thinking you are banking at the Bank of Heaven when, in reality, you've been banking at that other bank.

You may have spent your entire life thinking you are banking at the Bank of Heaven when, in reality, you've been banking at that other bank. You may think you've been operating like a Christian and have been doing so as a Babylonian. Here's how you can find out: a checklist of five indicators that you're banking at the wrong bank.

Sign #1: You've chosen a job or career over an assignment.

Jer. 1:5 says, "Before I formed thee in the belly I knew thee; and before thou camest forth out of the womb I sanctified thee, and I ordained thee a prophet unto the nations." Many other Scriptures tell us that even while you were in your mother's womb, you had an assignment. God sent you to this earth to fulfill a specific assignment. Jeremiah was sent to be a prophet. Samson was sent to deliver the Israelites from the Philistines. Jesus was sent to be the Savior of the world. You may have been sent to be a teacher or a musician or a missionary or an architect. You may have been sent to start a business that creates a service or product that blesses people's lives. Or God might have given you an assignment to be a lawyer to help defend those who would not have help if you weren't there.

So many people refuse to step into their calling because they're afraid they won't have provision if they do. "If I leave this job and do what God said, how am I going to eat? How am I going to be able to live?" That's what a Babylonian would say, and it's a sign that you're at the Bank of the World. Fear is keeping you in a job that you know you have no business being in. Are you picking your job and your career according to the money that comes from it, or are you picking it according to your God-given assignment? Babylonian.

What if God tells you to leave your career, and you have to take less money to do your assignment? In Genesis chapters 11 and 12, Abraham could have chosen to stay in Ur of the Chaldees and keep his job. He was doing well, and you would think that was his God-given assignment, but it wasn't. He chose it on his own, and when God said, "Leave and come here, and I'll provide for you," he did. It wasn't in Ur that Abraham became rich in every area. It was when he followed his assignment that God made him financially wealthy and blessed him, not only in his money, but in all things.

Sign #2: You refuse to return the tithe and give offerings.

If you don't tithe, perhaps one of the reasons is because you really don't believe God will provide for you. "If I give up that tithe, I won't be able to pay my rent." Babylonian! What a sign that you're not trusting the Bank of Heaven to give you withdrawals when you need it. You don't believe God will provide for you, so you are trying to do it yourself. You're operating according to the Bank of the World.

Deuteronomy chapter 26 shows that the very act of tithing is declaring that God is your Provider. You are saying, "God, I'm proving I believe You are my Provider by giving You the first 10 percent of what comes into my hands." If, on the other hand, you refuse to give it to Him, you are saying, "God, You are not my provider. The world is, and I am proving it by keeping that money in my hands." Babylonian. Instead of being that twelve-year-old kid on the street who finds a family that wants to adopt him and take care of him, you say "no" to the family. You stay on the street and just keep scrounging around trying to live while you could be provided for and have a different focus on life.

Luke 16:11 says, "If therefore ye have not been faithful in the unrighteous mammon, who will commit to your trust the true riches?" If you aren't faithful with the tithe, how are you going to get the anointing? Mal. 3:10 says:

> Bring ye all the tithes into the storehouse, that there may be meat in mine house, and prove me now herewith, saith the Lord of hosts, if I will not open you the windows of heaven, and pour you out a blessing, that there shall not be room enough to receive it.

Sign #3: You stay in a gray area financially.

Earlier we talked about different ways to get money—God's ways and the world's ways. The world's ways are not always righteous. Some of them are obviously sinful, and you may be scrupulous to avoid them, but there are plenty of gray areas—things that are honest in the sight of the world but dishonest in the sight of God. Do any of these sound a little close to home? Do you have bootleg cable coming into your home? Babylonian. How about DVDs on the shelf that weren't produced by the people that made the movie? Babylonian. Do you play the lottery and gamble that this week's cash jackpot is going to pay your electric bill? Babylonian. How about questionable business deals? Babylonian.

I would not even call these gray areas; they are out-and-out sin— but the world would call them gray. If any of them sounds familiar to you, you are banking at the wrong bank, and you are a Babylonian.

Sign #4: You over-rely on government or other organizations for your provision.

Do you rely on the government more than you do on God? Babylonian. The Bible says righteousness exalts a nation. If you pick government programs over righteousness, you are a Babylonian.

If you would actually elect someone to government who supports abortion, supports homosexual sin, supports things you know are against God because of his or her economic policy, you are a Babylonian. You may not like reading this, but go ahead and read Matthew chapter 18 and tell me what it says about how God feels about children. If we kill babies, what do you think God's reaction is? God is furious about the premeditated murder of His children. It is easily the number one issue in our country. It is the slavery of our day. It is worse than slavery.

If you are going to pick programs over righteousness, that is the Babylonian system. If government, not righteousness, is your source, you are a Babylonian. As far as God is concerned, if you seek Him first and His righteousness, He'll make sure all the other things are taken care of. If you are going to pick any civilization over God's civilization because you are hoping that civilization means you are taken care of, that is the Babylonian system.

Sign #5: You worry when the economy suffers.

You're stressed. You're worried. You're concerned. You're complaining. You're getting others stressed and worried and concerned. Babylonian! I'm not saying you should ignore what's happening around you, but I am saying you should respond in God's way, not your own. Phil. 4:6 says, "Be careful for nothing; but in every thing by prayer and supplication with thanksgiving let your requests be made known unto God." So if there is a problem, instead of worrying about it, God says, "Bring it to Me and thank Me for the answer. I will give you peace throughout that process, and I will take care of the problem."

How did you do with these five signs? I didn't make it a quiz, but you can grade yourself and see how many were a little too familiar. Maybe it's time to switch banks.

Are You Living Life 1.0 or Life 2.0?

S O WHOM ARE YOU RELYING UPON TO BE YOUR BANKER? TO whom are you making deposits? From whom are you making withdrawals? Part of what we're dealing with in our economy right now is banks failing; that is a good reason why you shouldn't let the world's system be your bank. I'm not talking about pulling all your money from a bank and keeping it under your pillow. I'm talking about where you put your trust, where you look to for your source of income, and whom you are relying upon to sustain you and provide for you.

You can't bank at the Bank of Heaven and the Bank of the World at the same time. It doesn't work that way.

Are you realizing you need to change banks? Is it time for you to have a new banker? Is it time to let Jesus be your Banker? That is one of the best ways you can recession-proof your future. Phil. 4:19 says, "But my God shall supply all your need according to his riches in glory by Christ Jesus." He is the only One who can give you access to the Bank of Heaven. Once you have access to Jesus as your Banker, when you need a house, the kingdom of God will pay for it. Need a car? The kingdom of God will pay for that. Want to start a business or need money to do something that God has told you to do? The kingdom of God will pay for it. But here's the condition: You need to allow Jesus to be your Banker. You have to let Him fill that role in your life. God wants to be your Banker. He wants to be the One who receives your deposits, the One from whom you withdraw, who pays for your house and your car, starts your business, and takes care of all your financial needs.

Many people realize they need God to be their Banker, but they're not ready to give up their old banker yet. You can't bank at the Bank of Heaven and the Bank of the World at the same time. It doesn't work that way. You can't get your provision out of heaven and at the same time get your provision out of the Babylonian system. You have to make a choice. In Matthew chapter 6, Jesus explains that you cannot bank at two locations at once. "No man can serve two masters: for either he will hate the one, and love the other; or else he will hold to the one, and despise the other. Ye cannot serve God and mammon" (v. 24).

The word *mammon* refers to wealth personified. It's really referring to money, to possessions, and, ultimately, to another god in the earth. In this chapter, Jesus is talking about your financial life, what you'll eat, what you'll drink, what you'll put on. Remember that we studied Jesus' admonition to "Seek ye first the kingdom of God . . .; and all these things shall be added unto you." We learned that He meant, "Don't worry about where you're going to get provision from. Don't worry about it! Take no thought about it."

You may be asking, "How am I going to pay for my mortgage?" That is a need, is it not? "How am I going to have transportation?" For most, that is a need. "How am I going to pay rent?" We could go on and on and on. God says, "Don't worry about these things. Don't worry about provision." This is how you operate when God is your Source, when Jesus is your Banker. You don't worry about these things.

In this chapter in Matthew, Jesus draws a contrast between operating in the world's financial system, where you make your withdrawals from the world's system and your deposits into the world's system, and the Bank of Heaven. If you do business at the Bank of the World, when you need money to get a house, you go to the world's system to get a loan so you can get that house. If you need a car, you go through the world's system to get a loan so you can get that car.

Jesus says, "For after all these things do the Gentiles seek" (v. 32). He's not saying those things are wrong. He's saying where you find them, where you seek them and go after them, can be wrong. His point is that you should have a different MO than the world, a different "method of operation" than the world has when it comes to receiving finances. Jesus is letting you know that the world is operating at a lower level of living. They are living Life 1.0, and you have the opportunity to live Life 2.0.

Again, He is not saying there is anything wrong with the things themselves, but what is wrong is that a major part of our lives can be spent pursuing the things of this world. These are people who have to operate without God's provision, without God helping them, without God providing for them—meaning they are on their own. That is Life 1.0.

Paul said, "No man that warreth entangleth himself with the affairs of this life; that he may please him who hath chosen him to be a soldier" (2 Tim. 2:4). When you are on a mission, you don't have a fit because you didn't go to McDonald's for lunch. You are not thinking about McDonald's. You are not upset because you didn't get to watch your favorite TV show. You're not thinking about those things. Those things are secondary. You are thinking about your number one priority: fulfilling that mission.

Jesus means that the number one priority of those who are without God is to make sure they have provision—whether it is just making sure their needs are met or going a step further and reaching after the riches of this world and all the things they believe riches will bring them. That is their mission.

Then He says, "You are different. You have a heavenly Father. They are fatherless, but you have a Father, and He knows. He knows!" The Bible says the eyes of the Lord are over the righteous. His eyes are on our land. The Lord has been mindful of us (see Psalm 115). He has you and your prosperity on His mind. He knows what you need before you ask Him. It's His job to make sure you don't have any lack.

Banking at the wrong bank will inevitably lead to failure. It may not come right away, but it will come. So what do Christians do when the world's system fails? If they made a decision to stay in that system and operate according to the world's system, they're going to go down with it. Frankly, that's why most Christians are struggling today. They may have been sitting in church and hearing messages like this and shouting "Amen! Hallelujah!"—but they never actually switched banks. So when their bank went down, they lost everything they had.

Is it too late? Can you still make a change and let God be your Banker? Is it too late to trust the One who is not impacted by what happens with the stock market? Who doesn't move when real estate prices do? The One whose bank is untouchable? The One who always has enough for you to finance that business enterprise or go on that missions trip?

Maybe you're reading this and thinking, "Yes, that's me. I've been a believer for years, but I banked at the wrong bank. The world's system has failed me, and now I'm in deep trouble. Is there any hope for me?"

Yes, there is, and tomorrow we're going to study practical ways to change banks.

Day 19

How to Change Banks

THE TITLE OF TODAY'S STUDY COULD BE "PRACTICAL WAYS to Recession-proof Your House"—because when you switch to the Bank of Heaven, you are well on your way to making your house recession-proof. You'll notice that each one of these practical ways we'll study today begins with the word "choose" because you really have a choice in the matter. God gives you free will, and you can choose whatever you want. In all these ways, you are saying, "God, I choose You as my Source. Jesus, I choose You as my Banker."

Remember, moving your account from the Bank of the World to the Bank of Heaven begins with a choice. You must choose not only *where* you bank, but *how* you bank. You can choose to do things God's way, or you can choose to continue in your own way. If you make the choice to bank at the Bank of Heaven, God will not only take care of your need, but He will ultimately get you to a place where you are enjoying the desires of your heart—and blessing many people as a result.

When you choose God's ways—the kingdom way—you don't worry when the economy suffers. Remember Psalm 112, which we looked at this week? "He shall not be afraid of evil tidings: his heart is fixed, trusting in the Lord" (v. 7). Whenever you turn on the news or open a newspaper nowadays, you are surrounded by "evil tidings" of gloom and doom, but when you make a choice to follow God's ways, He promises to make your house recession-proof.

Choose to Get Money God's Way

Earlier we learned there are various ways to get money; some are godly, and others are not. You must choose to get money God's way, according to His principles of righteousness.

There are a number of ways to become a millionaire. You can do it through crime if you are devious enough. You can become a millionaire through corruption. We're seeing some of that on Wall Street and in Washington right now. People are cheating the system and therefore cheating people out of their money—and they are walking away with millions. You also can become a millionaire by promoting sin. Think about the people who started pornographic magazines that are sold on newsstands today. They are multimillionaires, and they have made their millions by getting people entangled in sin. This is the case with many secular rap artists today. They are making millions from promoting sin and, ultimately, helping people go to hell.

You can make money the world's way—or you can do it God's way, in a respectable way. God is a Creator, and His Word says, "It is he that giveth thee power to get wealth" (Deut. 8:18). If you choose to get money God's way, you may need to make a decision to turn your back on some ways you have been making money. The devil will give you plenty of opportunity to continue, but ask the Holy Spirit for the strength to say no to them. Then ask Him what you can do to get money His way. He may give you a verse, such as Eph. 4:28, where you work with your hands and produce what is good. God can give you an idea that creates a service for mankind. So many people could use that service that you could become a millionaire. If you choose to get money God's way, He'll show you how—and in the process, you will recession-proof your house.

Choose to Seek First the Kingdom of God

When you do your banking at the Bank of the World, your entire focus is on seeking provision. As we've already seen, God gives you another directive—and if you choose to follow it, it will help you to recession-proof your house. The verse we've looked at many times, "Seek ye first the kingdom of God, and his righteousness" (Matt. 6:33), means you are seeking first to help God accomplish His purpose of saving the world by witnessing to unbelievers, discipling other believers, serving in your church and community, praying, giving, and more.

What happens if you do that? "All these things shall be added unto you" (v. 33). Now this is conditional. There's a big *if*. If you choose to do what He says, if you choose to seek first God's kingdom, if you join His campaign, if you choose to do everything you can to help Him grow His kingdom, in the process of doing that, you keep growing in Him. God says, "If you choose to seek My kingdom first, I'll make sure all these things shall be added unto you." *Shall* is the strongest assertion in the English language. You can't say it any stronger than that, so you have a kingdom-backed guarantee about your future that all these things *shall* be.

All refers to clothes, food, drink, mortgage, rent, car, education—not only for you, but for others. If you seek God, He will make sure you don't lack for any good thing. The book of Joel promises if you obey and serve Him, you will spend your days in prosperity and your years in pleasures. Isa. 1:19 says you will "eat ye that which is good, and let your soul delight itself in fatness."

Choose Your Assignment Over Your Job

Are you choosing a job and a career over an assignment? Is fear keeping you in a job that you know you have no business being in? If you realize you've chosen a job or your career over God's assignment for you, it is time to choose your assignment over your job. Now, I'm not telling you to run out and quit your job today. God has a plan and a path to get you to where you are supposed to be—and it begins by making a choice and telling Him, "God, I choose my assignment over my job. I choose You." Matt. 7:7 says, "If you seek Him, you will find Him" (paraphrased). James 1:5 promises if you ask God for wisdom, He will give it to you. He will direct you as to what to do and when to do it.[4]

Choose to Start Giving God the Tithe and Offerings

Remember the second sign that you are banking at the Bank of the World? You refuse to return the tithe and give offerings. So one of the primary ways you can switch banks is to give God your tithes and offerings. The owner of the Bank of the World will give you every reason why you shouldn't do this, particularly when the world is telling you the economy is tanking and you need to hold on to every penny you've got. What, however, does God promise you? We've quoted this verse before:

> Bring ye all the tithes into the storehouse, that there may be meat in mine house, and prove me now herewith, saith the Lord of hosts, if I will not open you the windows of heaven, and pour you out a blessing, that there shall not be room enough to receive it.
>
> Mal. 3:10

Remember, our goal is not just to have enough finances for ourselves, but also to bless others. Isn't that what God is promising you here? You have a choice. You can listen to CNN and Fox, you can read *The Wall Street Journal* and your local newspaper, and you can choose to believe that God can't prosper you in a time like this. Or you can choose to believe God, to take Him at His word. You can choose to say, "God, I'm sorry I've looked at what the world is going through and cut back on my giving and on my obedience to You. I ask You to be my Banker, and I'm going to show You I'm serious by giving my tithes and offerings." It's a choice.

Choose Righteousness

Let's look at Deut. 28:1: "And it shall come to pass, if thou shalt hearken diligently unto the voice of the Lord thy God, to observe and to do all his commandments which I command thee this day."

So one of the first things you have to do to be debt-free is keep God's commandments. We could spend pages on why we need to live holy in order to get out of debt. You cannot sleep around and live a sinful life, and still have the blessing work for you. You're not going to steal from people and have the blessing work for you. You're not going to cuss people out and gossip—and many other things you know are wrong—and have the blessing work for you. Why? Because you can't sow the wrong kind of seed and expect a good harvest. Your deeds are seeds, so if you sow the wrong kind of seed through behavior that's contrary to God's Word, you can't expect God to bring you a good harvest in the way of supernatural debt cancellation.

So Deut. 28:1 sets out the conditions for receiving the results of verse 12: "The Lord shall open unto thee his good treasure, the heaven to give the rain unto thy land in his season, and to bless all the work of thine hand: and thou shalt lend unto many nations, and thou shalt not borrow."

It's not the economy, not the government, not your job. Thank God for all those things, which He can use to bless you, but ultimately, He's the One who is your Source when you're banking at the Bank of Heaven. The word *shall,* we've already seen, is a strong word used to back the promise of God. If you do His Word, there's a kingdom-backed guarantee that this is what He'll do for you. "The Lord shall open to thee." If He's got to open it, it means it must have been closed. For people who aren't obeying the Word of God, it is closed. When they walk up to the Bank of Heaven, they see a "closed" sign on the door. You, on the other hand, walk right by that sign and walk in.

If you want to switch banks, you must make a choice only to do things that are absolutely, positively, without a doubt righteous when it comes to your finances.

Notice the Word is specific about whom He is opening the door for: "thee." In my Bible, I wrote, "He's going to open to me." What is He going to open to you? "His good treasure." The good news about His good treasure is that it's the same thing we read about in Phil. 4:19. "My God shall supply all your need according to his riches in glory by Christ Jesus." It's the blessing of the Lord that maketh rich.

Mal. 3:10 tells us He'll open the windows of heaven and pour out a blessing for you.

Choose Righteousness When It Comes to Finances

You should, of course, choose righteousness in all areas of your life, but in this book, we're specifically looking at choosing righteousness when it comes to finances—because it's easy to choose otherwise. This is similar to the first choice above—choosing to get money God's way—but it's important enough that I've listed it again in a slightly different way. If you want to switch banks, you must make a choice only to do things that are absolutely, positively, without a doubt righteous when it comes to your finances.

If you are in any kind of business, you know there are plenty of opportunities to cheat. If you are operating your business according to the world's system, chances are very good that at some point, you're going to do something that is kind of shady—something that's contrary to the Word of God—so that you can make money. The Bible talks about a false balance: "A false balance is abomination to the Lord: but a just weight is his delight" (Prov. 11:1). Are you paying your taxes? Are you declaring all your income (including tips)? Are you giving your employer 100 percent effort on the job (your earthly employer *and* your heavenly employer)? If not, you are cheating people out of money. You ultimately are pursuing the pride of life, the braggadocio of life. You are trying to get enough money to show those in the world you are better than they are. You drive down the street and turn your nose up at the folks next to you because you're driving a Bentley—the one you got by unrighteous means.

Prov. 1:32 says, "The prosperity of fools shall destroy them." So as long as you act like a fool with your money, God is not going to give you His prosperity. He'd rather have you at least saved and going to heaven, even if you go there broke, than see you have a lot of money and go to hell. We've already seen that the Bible says it's better to be righteous and poor than unrighteous and rich.

Is the Holy Spirit convicting you? Do you see areas where you've chosen to act in an unrighteous manner when it comes to your finances, where you have not managed your money as He says in His Word? If so, it's time to choose righteousness. You will not be sorry. The Lord will honor you for making that choice. His Word promises, "I have been young, and now am old; yet have I not seen the righteous forsaken, nor his seed begging bread" (Ps. 37:25). In fact, Ps. 34:9-10 makes a promise: If you fear God and choose to act righteously, He will make sure you don't lack for any good thing.

Choose Righteousness Over Government or Any Other Organization

When you bank at the Bank of the World, you rely on others, instead of God, to provide for you. That often can be the government or another organization. Who is your provider? Is it the U.S. Treasury? If so, that is the Bank of the World. You're in trouble because you've pushed God out of the equation. An overreliance on the government or any other organization is proof that you are a Babylonian.

If you rely on the government more than you rely on God, if you rely on your place of employment more than you rely on God, it's time for a change. Make a decision to choose righteousness over government in your voting or any other organization—and watch God come to your aid. You'll be banking at the Bank of Heaven, which has unlimited resources.

Choose to Get Out of Debt

Like all the other points in today's reading, this one begins with a choice. Debt is a key to doing business with the Bank of the World. Getting out of debt is one of the prime ways to move your account from that institution to the Bank of Heaven. In fact, getting out of debt is so critical that it deserves a week all its own.

Day 20

GROUP DISCUSSION

Action point: Let Jesus be your Banker.

Action Scripture: "I call heaven and earth to record this day against you, that I have set before you life and death, blessing and cursing: therefore choose life, that both thou and thy seed may live" (Deut. 30:19).

Action step: Pray and ask God specifically what your assignment from Him is. This may take you more time, but you can get started today.

Questions:

1. What did you read in our study this week that surprised you? That caused you to change how you thought about God and His

ways? That motivated you to continue on the twenty-eight-day challenge?

2. What are some financial gray areas that we as Christians need to avoid? Is there anything specific in your own life that the Holy Spirit has shined the light on this week? (You do not have to reveal anything confidential.)

3. Are you worried about the economy? Why or why not?

4. Do you know what your God-given assignment is?

5. What are the benefits of being on assignment?

6. What is the difference between living to give and living to get? Give some examples, including a person you know who lives to give. What benefits do you see in his or her life as a result of living this way?

Day 21

REST

CONTINUE TO MEDITATE ON WHAT YOUR SPECIFIC ASSIGN-ment from God might be.

Week 4

NO MORE DEBT

Day 22

DEBT: THE NEVER-
ENDING HOLE

O UR GOAL OF THIS FINAL WEEK OF THE CHALLENGE IS TO understand the gravity of debt and then to declare war on it. I want to remind you that your goal is to put yourself in a position that you are recession-proof. Those in the world around you may be struggling financially and losing their jobs, their savings, and their homes, but you want to be in a position where God has protected you from those things. You want to continue to take care of your family the way you've always wanted to—and not only to maintain, but actually increase during this time. You want this not just for yourself, but also to be a blessing to the world around you. Why?

Because according to John 15:8, when you bear much fruit, it gives glory to the Father.

Remember this as we tackle the subject of debt during our final week. It's not easy to face, but you need to do it in order to recession-proof your future. In fact, getting out of debt is the prime way to do that. The Bank of the World runs on credit (or debt). This is nothing new, as we see from Neh. 5:1-5. The people mortgaged their land, vineyards, and houses so they could have money to buy corn. Then they mortgaged other things to have money to pay their taxes. Does that sound familiar?

The world's system has been designed by individuals who've found a clever way to make money: They get people into debt and then have them spend the rest of their lives trying to pay it off—all with interest, of course. So when they come to the end of their lives, instead of having money saved up to enjoy life, they have to borrow even more.

God's will is that you are in a position where you can live on cash. I know the economic models that business schools teach will tell you the opposite—that you get more leverage if you live off credit. There are two sides to that story, however, and they never want to talk about the other side. Sure, you get more leverage for a while, but what happens when the house of cards falls? What happens when you can't make a payment? All that leverage means nothing then. It's better just to do it God's way. And God's way, ultimately, is debt-free. I'm not telling you it is a sin to be in debt, but it is not God's best for you.

Let's look at Deuteronomy chapter 28, which we touched on last week. This chapter spells out God's guarantee to you when you bank at the Bank of Heaven. One of the blessings for doing business there is that "thou shalt lend unto many nations, and thou shalt not borrow" (v. 12). If you are lending to someone, that means you don't just have enough; that means you have more than enough. You've got something extra to let somebody else use for a while.

It doesn't stop there. You'll "lend unto *many*" (emphasis added). If you're lending to many, you don't have just a little something extra; you've got an abundance. You've got so much, in fact, that you can send it out to lots of different people. You can let lots of folks borrow that money, and it's not going to have any kind of impact on your financial life. You are so blessed that you can just send out money, and it won't have any negative impact on your own life.

He's talking about Israel as a nation here, but for them to get to this place as a nation, they had to get to this place individually. And that's the promise of God for you. You see the same kind of promise in Deuteronomy chapters 15 and 16. You'll lend to many. You'll reign over other nations. You'll reign in the financial arena. You'll be the head and not the tail. You'll be the richest nation in the world.

It's interesting to study this Scripture because this is exactly how the United States became the United States. America is great because America is good. That's how we became the most prosperous nation—because we were the nation that was the closest to the Word of God. We obeyed the Word more than any other nation. And that's why we became the head and not the tail, and why we reign over other nations, why we're the world's only superpower, because of the blessing that has been on this nation. Now, of course, all that's in jeopardy. This nation has been sliding in the wrong direction for a long time, but America got here because of those principles.

God's promise to you is that you will not borrow. You will be the head, not the tail. When I read that, I wrote in my Bible, "My borrowing days are over." I wrote that because I could see that the will of God is for me to be the lender and not the borrower. Never, ever again would I have to borrow a penny. You may be saying, "Well, one day I'll get to that, Pastor." No! Today is the day! This is the day you draw the line and say, "I'm going to use my God-given faith to access the blessing, and I'll never have to borrow again—because the will of God is not for me to be the borrower; the will of God is for me to be the lender. In fact, the will of God is that I step up to an even higher destiny than that and be the giver!"

As I write this book, the housing market has crashed, and the stock market is plummeting. People who are living on credit are worried about their investments, but people who live on cash are able to increase during this time—because they're the ones with the money to buy stocks and homes that are priced way below their value. Can you see how God can increase you while the world around you is decreasing? You have to put yourself in the position ahead of time where you're able to do that. If you're in debt, you can't.

Benefit of Living Without Debt

There is a benefit to living a life without debt. My wife's grandfather was a wise man, who bought a lot of land and gave it to his children to build on. It's still in the family, and my wife owns some of it. (I should say we own some of it; I married into a rich family!) The land is about forty-five minutes outside of New Orleans, about halfway between that city and Baton Rouge. When Hurricane Katrina hit New Orleans, and a few years later Hurricane Gustav hit Baton Route head-on, thousands of homes were destroyed; people who were already living on credit were devastated, as their money, which was tied up in their mortgaged homes, was suddenly worthless. If you relied on being able to go to the bank to withdraw money or even use a credit card to do it, you were in trouble because power was out for days. You needed to have some cash on hand. People who had cash on hand were king.

If you live off credit, you could find yourself not having money when you need it. If the system fails, you will be in financial trouble.

Years' and even decades' worth of investment could be gone. Let's make it a little more personal. If you have children who want to go to college, but you know they can't go because you can't pay for it because you're still paying off a house, what does that tell you about debt? Or you may be able to afford college, but not the one you want your child to go to; the one you can afford teaches ungodly principles, but the one that teaches the values you believe in is out of your price range. So you have to make the decision where to send your child not based on what's best for your child, but on what's in your bank account. Your child's future is based on the fact that you are in debt. I know that's not what you want for your child.

Prov. 22:7 says, "The rich ruleth over the poor, and the borrower is servant to the lender." When you take out a thirty-year loan from the bank to buy a house, you are a servant to the bank. They now get a percentage of your work life. You have to work for them, in essence, to pay back what you borrowed from them. If you don't, they can sue you, and depending on the circumstances, you might end up in jail. You have become a slave to the borrower.

Jesus died for you. He shed His blood, went to hell, and rose again so that you would no longer have to be in bondage. Do you think God wants you to be enslaved again by becoming a borrower? "If the Son therefore shall make you free, ye shall be free indeed" (John 8:36). You are free from Satan, free from the things of this world. So why on earth would you turn around and become a slave to the things of this world? Now, I want you to notice what I'm saying. I'm not saying it's sin to be in debt, but I am telling you it's not God's best for you, and here's why: The borrower is servant to the lender. The borrower is a slave to the lender.

Debt Is the Enemy

Debt is a problem, not just in the United States, but also in the body of Christ.

- A whopping 90 percent of the body of Christ is in debt.
- The average American adult has four credit cards in his or her wallet.
- Those credit card companies are charging 19 percent interest or more.
- Forty-three percent of American families spend more than they earn.
- Fifty percent of Americans pay only a minimum amount on their credit card payments.
- The average debt for an American is $8,000.
- Personal bankruptcies have doubled in the past decade.
- Ninety-six percent of Americans will retire dependent on government and family.
- Two percent of homes are actually paid for.
- Ninety-two percent of a family's disposable income is spent paying debt.
- Fifty-one billion dollars was spent on credit or debit cards in 2006.
- The number one cause of divorce in the United States is financial problems.

Do we need any clearer signs that debt is the enemy? It destroys marriages, it damages credibility, it drives people to stress, bankruptcy, suicide, and murder. Debt hinders believers from being able to fully finance the gospel. What's the most important thing to God right now? It is helping people hear the truth about Jesus and leading them into a relationship with Jesus. God's desire is for all men to hear the gospel, be saved, and come into the knowledge of the truth. And so He puts money into the hands of His saints so they can help finance the preaching of the gospel.

There are millions of people who have yet to receive Jesus—and your money can assist ministries and churches in winning them. What keeps most Christians from giving when they want to give? Their debt. They're so busy working for whomever they're in debt to that they don't have the extra income to help win people's lives.

If debt is the enemy, then you don't need to have it in your house. You need to declare about debt, "Not in my house." You need to treat debt in your house as you would treat a fire if it broke out in your house. If a fire broke out in your house, would you sit down and watch television? Would you pick up a book? Would you go to sleep? If a fire broke out in your house, your priority at that moment would be to stamp out the fire whatever way you could—because that fire is going to bring about great damage to your house.

If there's debt in your house, you must make it your absolute priority to pay it off and get rid of it. Declare war! Don't allow yourself to get distracted!

When you have a debt, God expects you to pay it off. Bankruptcy is not a biblically acceptable option. In Exodus chapter 22, God says if a man borrows from his neighbor, make sure he pays that man what he owes. Ezekiel says a godly man makes sure he pays the pledges that he's made to the debtor; he pays him back. That is the honorable and godly thing to do. It is not honorable and godly to use the government to give you back pennies on the dollar. If you do that, you are sowing the wrong kind of seed, and you're going to get the kind of harvest you don't want to have. It's going to come back and impact your financial life later—and I'm not talking about just your credit report. Debt in your house can destroy your marriage, your credibility, your health, and more.

I'm here to incite you to war—to declare war on debt. If there's debt in your house, you must make it your absolute priority to pay it off and get rid of it. Declare war! Don't allow yourself to get distracted! I'm here to get you to pull out your Holy Ghost gun, put on your armor, and say, "Debt, I'm coming after you. I'm taking you out. And when I get you out of my house, you will never, ever come back again. I'm not going to stop there. I'm going to chase you out of other people's houses, too, because I'm going to help them get out of debt. Debt, I declare war on you!"

If the Holy Spirit is convicting you to join this war, say this prayer with me: "God, I have been wrong to get into debt. I see it now, and I repent. I know that debt is not part of a biblical worldview or how You want me to live life. It's hindered me from helping You reach the lost. With Your help, I'm going to get my Holy Ghost fire extinguisher, pick up my foot, and stamp this debt out of my house so that I can be debt-free and help You do what You want to do on this earth! Debt? Not in my house!"

Day 23

How to Win the War on Debt

YESTERDAY YOU DECLARED WAR ON DEBT. YOU MADE A GREAT decision. Getting out of debt won't happen by good intentions alone, however. During this final week of our study, we're going to cover specific action steps you can take to win the war on debt. This book is very practical. It is not a book of theory or something to make you say, "Amen, Pastor Andre. That's good preaching." My goal is to give you specific steps you can take to recession-proof your house. Ready to begin?

Getting out of debt won't happen by good intentions alone.

1. Tithe faithfully.

Last week we learned that one of the ways to stop doing business with the Bank of the World and to start banking at the Bank of Heaven is to give God the tithe. Hopefully, you chose to do that. Tithing is the first thing you've got to do to declare war on debt. Mal. 3:8 says, "Will a man rob God? Yet ye have robbed me. But ye say, Wherein have we robbed thee? In tithes and offerings." Tithe, of course, means "tenth." It's the first 10 percent of all of your increase.

The prophet goes on to say that if you rob God, "Ye are cursed with a curse" (v. 9). The curse is the opposite of the blessing. Blessing is an empowerment from heaven to cause you to prosper. The curse is an empowerment from hell that causes you to fail. It sabotages you. When you're under the curse, God is not able to increase you. If you've made a choice to bank at the Bank of the World, remember it is ultimately run by president Satan.

The tithe is holy unto the Lord (see Lev. 27:30), and you can't mishandle holy things and expect God to bless you. Remember what happened to the Israelites who mishandled the ark of the covenant; they actually lost their lives. If you mishandle the tithe, you deal with the curse.

Notice the progression of what God promises to do once you bring the tithe:

Bring ye all the tithes into the storehouse, that there may be meat in mine house, and prove me now herewith, saith the Lord of hosts, if I will not open you the windows of heaven.

Mal. 3:10

So the implication is if you don't bring the tithe, the windows of heaven are closed to you. Once you bring the tithe, God promises to pour out a blessing on you so great that there won't be room enough to receive it. Abraham gave a tithe, and then God said, "I'm your exceeding great reward."

Haggai chapter 1 talks about what happened to Israel:

Is it time for you, O ye, to dwell in your cieled houses, and this house lie waste? Now therefore thus saith the Lord of hosts; Consider your ways. Ye have sown much, and bring in little; ye eat, but ye have not enough; ye drink, but ye are not filled with drink; ye clothe you, but there is none warm; and he that earneth wages earneth wages to put it into a bag with holes. Thus saith the Lord of hosts; Consider your ways.

Vv. 4-7

God said, "Look, you left My house in ruin. You've built your own houses. So now when you go to work, you're bringing in money, but you're putting it in a bag with holes in it." Have you ever experienced that? You take a drink, but it's not filling you up. You eat food, but it's not filling you up. You buy clothes, but they're not enough. Why? You're living under the curse because you're not taking care of God's business first.

Let me be frank with you. You can get out of debt by following just natural means, but we're believing God for supernatural debt cancellation as we've seen God do throughout the Bible. We believe that can happen because we're banking at the Bank of Heaven, and He's going to help us pay off our debt. He's going to do it in a quicker fashion. It's going to be accelerated and done without toil. It's going to be without sweat. But for that to happen, you've got to live under open windows—and you can't live under open windows if you're not tithing. If you want to take a shower, you cannot get wet if you are standing by the sink instead of under the showerhead. Do you want God to bless you and increase you? Do you want Him to help you get out of debt? You've got to tithe.

2. Give bountifully.

One of the things I've learned as a pastor is that people have to do the basics. Most people, however, don't. They immediately want to get into all the deep stuff, but if you don't do the basics, it doesn't matter how much you know. Giving bountifully is a basic. Prov. 11:24 says, "There is that scattereth, and yet increaseth; and there is that withholdeth more than is meet, but it tendeth to poverty." Scattering talks about giving. It means you're giving in many places, not just to one person or one church. It also means you're giving a lot. It's not just a little here and a little there. It's bountiful giving. It's similar to 2 Cor. 9:8, which we've read before.

Chances are very good that you are going to need to see some financial increase in your life in order to get out of debt. For some people, it will just be a matter of cutting expenses, but most people need some kind of boost in revenue to get out of debt, particularly debt that includes the typical twenty- or thirty-year house loan.

God is saying that in order for you to increase, you have to scatter. So now you're not just talking about giving a tithe to your local church, but you're also talking about giving bountifully. Tithing is just the first fruits (see Prov. 3:9). Offering is the seed. If you sow sparingly, you'll reap sparingly. If you sow bountifully, you'll reap bountifully. You can actually determine, in some ways, the speed of your debt cancellation because if you just sow sparingly, it'll come in sparingly. You'll be able to chip away at your debt, but you probably want to take big chunks out of it. If so, you've got to sow bountifully. The return will come back to you bountifully and in chunks, and you'll pay off that debt in chunks.

Luke 6:38 says, "For with the same measure that ye mete withal it shall be measured to you again." So the more you scatter, the more you increase. That's so different from how the world thinks, but it's true. The tithe opens the windows of heaven, but the offering starts the flow of the blessing according to what you give.

Jesus referred in Mark chapter 12 to the woman who gave only two mites. He said she gave more than all the rich people. They gave more when it came to numbers, but she gave more when it came to percentage. That was bountiful giving. When you do that, you get drenched with the power of God. The Bible calls it burden-removing, yoke-destroying power (see Isa. 10:27). There is an anointing that will remove the burden of those extra bills, that will destroy the yoke—the bondage of that debt. Indeed, the blessing of the Lord maketh rich. Now when you're giving bountifully, you'll increase more and more and accomplish your goal of becoming debt-free.

Matt. 7:12 says, "Whatever you want others to do for you, you should do for them" (paraphrase). What a great way to get out of debt! Help someone else get out of debt. Gal. 6:10 says, "As we have therefore opportunity, let us do good unto all men." He goes on to say that when you're doing good to all men, particularly believers, you put yourself in a position to reap a harvest from every seed. In due season, you will reap. Ask God, "Whom do You want me to help get out of debt?" It may not be a person; it may be a ministry.

A minister wrote in one of his books about how he got hold of this principle. He was believing God for a car, and the Lord led him to an individual and told him to pay off the car. He wrote the person a letter, and they set it up so that he paid it every month for almost a year. A few months later, somebody walked up to him and gave him a car, free and clear.

In all these verses, there's nothing that indicates you're to stop giving just because the world is concerned about the economy struggling. You don't operate according to the world's financial system. If you decide to go from "he that scattereth" to "he that withholdeth," you will create your own recession.

3. Know what you owe.

When I say, "Know what you owe," I don't just mean the amount of money you owe, but the details about it. Prov. 27:23 says, "Be thou diligent to know the state of thy flocks, and look well to thy herds." *Diligent* means "to be constant in effort." You should be constant in giving your best effort toward knowing the state of your finances. In the Old Testament, that meant flocks, as in the Proverbs verse. Today that means our financial affairs. God is saying, "Know the state of your financial life." Whether you're an employer or an employee, you have your own personal business. You have to run your household like a business. You must have an idea of what's coming in and what's going out. You ought to sit down at least every week with your spouse and discuss what's happening financially and what changes you may need to make so your business is successful.

As an athlete, I learned playing basketball that the coach expected me to be diligent every single moment of every single drill every day. That's how you must be with your finances. How can you develop a strategy to get rid of debt if you don't really know what the debt is or even the terms of the debt? Make a list of your liabilities. How much do you owe? List every single thing that you owe. How much do you owe on your car? On your house? To your credit card companies? List the debt, the interest rate, and the term. Then make a list of your assets; how much do you own? You might think you don't own a thing, but you do. You own that TV, that couch, that department store you call a hall closet. You'd be surprised how much you own. (And you'd be surprised how much a good garage sale will get you.)

This may sound like a lot of work, but you don't win war without a strategy. If you don't even know what you owe, how are you going to develop a strategy to get rid of it? It may take you a few hours to compile this information; it may take you an entire Saturday. You'll have to pull out all those disgusting papers from the bank and car loan company, and you'll have to wade through all of them. There may be some details that are simply too painful to look at. You might be thinking, *Pastor, I'm out of faith on this one. If I look at this stuff long enough, I'm not going to be able to believe God for anything.*

You need to know. You will pay it off, but you have to know how much you've got to pay off. Make an appointment with yourself for some time this week when you'll do this, and then put it down on your calendar.

4. Develop a household budget.

When Prov. 27:23 says, "And look well to your herds," it doesn't mean to kind of watch them briefly; watch them carefully. Pay attention to what happens with them because you want them to stay healthy. Your herds refer to your finances. It's like a parent with a child. Our children are five years old, two years old, and three months old. Our two-year-old is so energetic that she's oblivious to her strength; when she's around the baby, we have to protect the baby, literally! I have to tell the two-year-old over and over again, "Be careful!" but she doesn't always get it, so I have to be on guard and make sure the baby is protected.

If you watch kids, you're supposed to pay attention to them so they can stay healthy. You should do the same thing with your finances. You've got to pay attention to what's going on, with the goal of making sure your finances stay healthy. One of the things that will help you do this is a household budget. Prov. 22:29 says, "Seest thou a man diligent in his business? he shall stand before kings; he shall not stand before mean men." You need to be diligent in running your household; that means having a budget and counting the costs. Then you'll know not just what you owe, but also how much is coming in and how much is going out—to the penny.

There's a large billboard in Atlanta that simply says, "Act your wage." You don't just develop a budget and forget about it. You then regularly—every week or so—look at what you spent and how it compares to what you've budgeted. You might say, "That's not what I intended to spend," so you make corrections to stay within your budget.

> If you'll properly manage what He's giving you now, then He knows He can trust you with more.

When I preach this message, it always gets real quiet around this point. When I talk about declaring war on debt, everyone shouts and cheers and is ready to enlist—but when I start talking about developing a budget and sticking to it, no one wants to hear that!

The Bible says, "He that is faithful in that which is least is faithful also in much: and he that is unjust in the least is unjust also in much" (Luke 16:10). In other words, if you'll properly manage what He's giving you now, then He knows He can trust you with more, and the anointing will begin to work. One of the things that will hinder the blessing in your life is not properly managing what God has already given you. So you must make sure you are properly managing it. God determines what He's going to give His believers based on their management skills. The parable of the talents shows that. In Matthew chapter 25, we see a man who represents God. He's a rich man, seemingly, who is going away for a long time. He takes five talents, gives it to one man; two talents, gives it to another; one talent, gives it to another. How did he decide that one man gets five but another gets only one? What criteria did he use? The Bible said he did it according to their own ability. He has watched these men, and he knows that the first one is living more faithfully than the second, and the second one is living more faithfully than the last one. So based on their faithfulness, he says, "I can trust this one with five. I can trust this one with two. I can trust this one with one."

Which one are you? Are you the one-talent man who doesn't even have a budget? Are you the one whom God can't even trust to tithe? Or maybe you're a two-talent man who does tithe and give, but you don't really pay attention to what's happening in your finances. Or are you the five-talent man who tithes, gives offerings, knows what you owe, has a budget, and lives within your means? You're the one God knows He can trust with more money. He knows that what you're doing right now is what you'll do on the days to come and in the years to come as your revenue increases. Prosperity destroys the fool. So as long as you act like a fool, God is not going to give you His prosperity because the Bible says it's better to be righteous and poor than unrighteous and rich.

What did God expect those men to do with the talents He gave them? He expected them to take those talents and manage them in such a way that they grew. Properly managing your money includes having a budget. You could really change your entire financial life in a matter of a few hours if you decide to take next Saturday afternoon to sit down and put a budget together. You would have a much clearer picture of where you are and a strategy to get you out of debt. I'm here to tell you that you have to do that to get out of debt. It doesn't happen by accident. Success is never by accident. It is always on purpose. Doing this will help you to realize how you are spending your money and what you're spending it on. Are you lusting after the things of the world? Are you wanting that big-screen TV just to be able to boast about it? To keep up with the neighbors? You might think, *Everyone has that new phone; I've got to get one.*

Having a budget will help you to learn to delay your gratification. We are living in a society that teaches us to want everything now. We pull up to a drive-through window, and they happen to take two minutes instead of one, and we say, "I'm never coming back here." We hate waiting. But that's the world's system. God's system teaches that through faith and patience, we obtain the promises. If you've got to have it now, there's something wrong.

A few years ago, I really, really, really wanted to finish my basement. I really wanted a media room badly. And I wanted it finished before football season. I wanted a big-screen TV so I could go down there and not have to hear kids while I was watching a game. I wanted to watch football and scream at the top of my lungs. My wife thinks there's something wrong with me. "Why can't you just sit in the chair and be quiet? Why do you have to talk to the TV?"

I wanted a place where I could yell and scream and throw something if I wanted to. And that, to me, was a nice finished basement with a brand-new media room. So one day my wife and I were in the mall, and we came across a new basement system. The salesmen said they could put it in our basement. I really didn't have anything in my spirit that was giving me a green light, but I said, "Let's just go in the store and talk with them." We spent an hour in there while they talked to us and talked and talked. It was grievous, but I didn't get the hint.

Finally, they made an appointment to come over to the house, and the sales pitch continued from there. My wife kept pulling me aside, telling me to ask them to leave, but I thought, *I can't do that. That's rude.* Finally, it reached the place where God said to me, "Why are you in so much of a hurry? You've got to have it now? Slow down. You don't need it right now."

I realized that this media room was not the key to my happiness. I was already happy; I have Jesus. Thankfully I didn't make a mistake and splurge on this basement. I was actually even considering a loan to do it. The Lord helped me to see it wasn't that important. And it wasn't what He wanted me to do.

Debt allows us to live a lifestyle for which we're not financially ready. It allows us to fulfill lust, and it's lust that causes us to be in a position of lack. The curse of poverty always comes as a result of bad choices. "I have set before you life and death, blessing and cursing: therefore choose life" (Deut. 30:19).

If you listen to God, you'll be safe, you'll do well, and you'll get out of debt. If you don't, and you continue to get what you want when you want it, you'll continue to live in debt. Stop adding debt to what you already owe. Borrow no more.

Day 24

DEBT-REDUCTION STRATEGIES

R EMEMBER WHAT WE LEARNED YESTERDAY: GETTING OUT OF debt won't happen by good intentions alone. During our final week of study, we're covering specific action steps you can take to win the war on debt. Let's continue.

5. Change how you think about money.

God will not wipe out your debt until you change your mind-set about money. Rom. 12:2 says, "And be not conformed to this world: but be ye transformed by the renewing of your mind." You renew your mind by consuming the Word of God, listening to it, reading it, meditating on it, and receiving revelation. Revelation brings renewal in your thinking. When thoughts come your way that are contrary to God's Word, you've got to cast them down.

You have to change your thinking about money from the way everyone else in the world thinks about it to the way God thinks about it. There are two types of thinking when it comes to money: prosperous thinking and poverty thinking. Did you ever notice that you never see "cash your check here" stores in affluent areas? Those companies have learned how to prey on the poor. You usually see those stores right next to a liquor store because the poor are the ones who are going to visit that liquor store. You don't see them where rich people are because rich people don't cash checks; they deposit them. Poor people cash checks.

 Prosperous thinking says, "I'm going to make money work for me."

Furniture stores advertise debt in the form of free credit: "Don't pay anything until January 2010." My wife and I did that once; we bought a big-screen TV and were so excited because we didn't have to pay until a year after the TV arrived in our house. *What a great deal,* we thought. We were just stupid. It's not that our parents and grandparents didn't try to teach us. There are just some things you don't get through your head until you make the mistakes yourself. We didn't realize that we were accumulating debt and interest; we ended up having to pay big for that thing. Thank God, He provided, and we learned.

Let's talk about prosperous thinking versus poverty thinking. Prosperous thinking says, "I'm going to make money work for me."

Some people argue there is some good debt, which is debt that makes you money. For example, some people think good debt is buying a house because over time, it should make you money. I'm not going to say there isn't such a thing as good debt, but I think we've seen enough in Scripture to say that it's really not God's best. The point is that prosperous people have their money make more money for them; they invest. Poverty thinking doesn't invest; it spends. Poverty thinking goes out and spends and gets bad debt—debt that just consumes, like debt for furniture. Or like financing an automobile because when the tires leave the lot and hit the pavement, the value of that vehicle just plummeted. Poverty thinking thinks quantity. Prosperous thinking thinks quality.

When someone with poverty thinking gets money, he or she thinks about spending it for entertainment. Have you ever noticed that some of the poor usually have a really good time? They are partying, drinking their forties, doing drugs, buying the best clothes. They run around with designer clothes and $150 gym shoes, and then they're mad at somebody else who has success because that person saved his or her money.

Someone with poverty thinking gets money and immediately thinks "entertainment," but someone with prosperous thinking gets money and immediately thinks "education." "I'm going to use that money to get some education and learn something. I'm going to buy a book. I'm going to go to school. I'm going to take a class."

If you realize you need to change the way you think about money, you may need to increase your financial literacy. There are classes you can take and books you can read and ministries that will mentor you on this. (See, for example, the list of resources in the back of this book.)

6. Use debt-reduction strategies.

God gave the widow in 2 Kings chapter 4 a debt-reduction strategy that enabled her to pay off her debt quickly. She was desperate, poor, a widow, a mother of a starving child, and faced with enormous debt and no way to pay it off. Elijah gave her a directive—gather some pots—and God miraculously provided enough oil so she could sell it and pay off all her debts.

That was wonderful, and God sometimes does that—but you will not always eliminate your debt in one fell swoop. You may be believing God for a $300,000 check to pay off all your debt—and that may happen—but it may not happen that way, either. In fact, we don't know how quickly the woman was able to sell off the oil and pay her debt.

While we ought to believe God for chunks, He may choose to do it otherwise. Think of the miracle of the loaves and fishes (see John chapter 6). Jesus expected them to be diligent and gather up every crumb and fish bone that still had any meat on it. When they did, they had twelve baskets full of scraps. Jesse Duplantis says, "Your treasures are in your fragments." It's not always the huge chunk.

When my wife and I first married, I'd come home with change in my pocket and would put it on the nightstand. She'd always grab it and put it into a jar. I thought it was kind of funny and, to be honest, a waste of time. After all, it was just a few pennies and nickels here and there. She'd just ignore me and keep on doing it, and I'd tease her about it. One day we went to the grocery story, and she pulled out a big jar full of change. I still didn't think it was much. She poured it into one of those machines that counts your change, and it was forty dollars or fifty dollars! I was so excited, but she said, "You're not getting any of this! You've been messing with me all this time; it's mine now." She had a revelation of doing a little bit by a little bit, and it all added up. That was a debt-reduction strategy.

John Avanzini, the apostle of finance, wrote a book called *Rapid Debt Reduction Strategies,* and it has impacted me greatly. He's been helping people for thirty years, so he knows what he's talking about. I want to share with you some of his principles, which will help you to pay off your house, your car, your credit cards, and whatever other debt you have.

1.   Treat all your debt as one big bill. When you come up with your list of what you owe, instead of looking at it as fifty dollars a month to the furniture store, $5,000 a year toward the car loan, and $20,000 for the school loan, add it all together and come up with what you must pay in total every month. That way you'll have one bill of, let's say, $1,000. That means you must pay $1,000 a month toward your debt reduction.

2.   Move your debt from high-interest accounts to lower-interest accounts, if possible. Let's say you've got some serious credit card debt with a number of cards. One company is charging you a much higher interest rate than the others. If possible, you want to move the debt of that card to a card that's charging less interest. If you can do that, you just saved money, and it didn't cost you a dime. You may want to consider getting a second mortgage on your home and using that to pay off all those credit cards; that is a smart strategy because the interest rate on the second mortgage will be a lot less than the interest rates of your credit cards. It may cost you a little, but you'll save money. This only works if you work diligently to pay off the second mortgage; you are still in debt, but your interest charges will be lower.

3.   Find a piece of money. You may be saying, "If I could do that, I wouldn't have this problem." This goes back to the second list you compiled above: How much do you owe? You might be surprised that there are things you can do to reduce your debt. What did the man of

God say to the woman in 2 Kings chapter 4? The first thing he asked her was, "What do you have in the house?"

A few years ago, a member of our church asked us to help her with finances. She wanted us to give her a few thousand dollars. We said to her just what Elijah asked the widow: "What do you have in your house?" She had a very expensive painting worth a couple thousand dollars. We told her we couldn't give her very much anyway and suggested she sell the painting and use the money for her need. Now, if someone's house burned down and he or she literally had nothing, of course we would come up with the money for that person, and we have for circumstances like that in our years in ministry—but her need was not that desperate. And she had something in her house that she could sell.

Her response? She made it quite clear that she did not want to sell the painting. She valued it so much that she wanted the church to take the money that was given to us to preach the gospel and instead give it to her to take care of her debt—so that she could keep the painting. When we did not pay off her debt, she got upset and left the church.

 Start really looking at what you're spending every month, and you're going to find some things you can cut back on.

Sometimes your piece of money is already sitting there. Other times you can find it simply by cutting back on some of the things you're doing right now. How often do you eat out? How much do you spend? When you put together a budget, you'll start to see some of this spending that you could direct toward debt repayment. Do you have to have a maid come in every week? Maybe you can get by with every other week. Maybe you don't get your hair done every single week; maybe you get it done every other week. Maybe you mow your own lawn. Do you have to have a new dress or a new suit for every new event? Every time? That's poverty thinking. You're spending your money on entertainment and on things that really aren't as important.

Start really looking at what you're spending every month, and you're going to find some things you can cut back on. This is where you find out the level of your commitment to this war. Are you really serious about getting out of debt? Are you ready to delay your gratification long enough to get out of debt?

4. When you find some money, pay off your smallest debt. Perhaps you're paying the minimum payment on everything else, but there may be a small debt that you can start paying off. It may happen in a week, or a few months, or a year, but focus on that debt and pay it off. Stop letting it accrue interest, especially if it's a really small debt. You might sell something (see number 3 above) and use that money to pay it off. That will help you get rid of that interest payment, too, because you're not just paying what you owe, but paying more toward it.

Then once you've paid it off, have a little celebration. Now, that does not mean go splurge more money, but do something to acknowledge the milestone you've just accomplished.

5. Take the money you were paying toward the debt that you just paid off, and use that same amount to pay off another debt. The temptation is to take that money and say, "Now I've got extra money to spend." That's poverty thinking. Take that money and apply it to either the next smallest debt or to the highest rate—whichever one you can pay off the fastest.

Let's say you put fifty dollars a month toward paying off a certain debt and one hundred dollars a month toward another. When you finish paying off the first debt, take that fifty dollars and add it to the one hundred dollars-per-month payment. Now you're paying $150 toward that debt. When you pay that off, you take the $150 per month and combine it with another monthly payment; let's say that one was fifty dollars, so now you're putting $200 toward it.

You see why it's important to treat your debt as if it's one big bill. Over time you'll start paying off all these debts. Soon you'll be left with nothing but your car note and your home mortgage. If you take the amount you were paying toward all your debt—say $1,000 a month—and apply it to your car note, imagine how quickly you'll knock that out! Once you get rid of that, you start applying it to your house note. Soon you'll be debt-free.

Day 25

CREDIT CARDS

TODAY WE'RE CONTINUING OUR LOOK AT SPECIFIC ACTION steps you can take to win the war on debt.

7. Get rid of credit cards.

Some people can have credit cards and handle them. Most cannot. I'll be real frank with you and tell you that my wife and I don't have credit cards. We haven't had one since the first year of our marriage. We heard Dr. Leroy Thompson talk about putting your credit cards in the freezer, and we literally did that. In fact, we forgot they were there. We decided we were not going to live off credit, and instead, we have a charge card. That is what credit cards used to be—where you have to pay it off in thirty days. With that kind of arrangement, you're not going to spend too much because you know in thirty days, you've got to pay it off. You can still abuse that just as you can abuse a debit card, but it comes with a lot more accountability.

You max out your card to the limit, and about that time, an offer comes in the mail. Surprise, you're preapproved for a card— with an even higher limit.

When you have a credit card, you find reasons to fill it up. You max out your card to the limit, and about that time, an offer comes in the mail. Surprise, you're preapproved for a card—with an even higher limit. *What an honor,* you think. You must have really good credit for them to do that. You fill up that card, and by now, you're in the lust of the flesh. Your interest rates are no longer the enticing introductory rates they were at the beginning. You pay minimum payments, but the finance charges are so high that you're actually going deeper into debt each month.

You don't have to have a credit card. Get a charge card. Or you can have a check card or a debit card, which limits you to the amount of money in your checking account. Either way, you need to have rules that you don't break because those things will still tear you up. The main rule is that if you have a charge card, you will always pay off the balance each month. When new offers and cards arrive in the mail, cut them up and destroy them.

And even if you have a charge card or debit card, you still may want to put it in the freezer. Just let it thaw out when you need it. The chances are pretty good you won't use it too often.

8. Beware of variable interest rates.

As I write this book, variable interest rates are in the news because of the havoc they have caused in banking institutions and personal finances across the country. Adjustable-rate mortgages (ARMs) can be dangerous, as many people have found out the hard way. If you have an ARM, you ought to be minding your p's and q's because you could easily get burned. Many people are losing their homes and their life savings.

9. Pay off your home loan as soon as you can.

No matter what kind of mortgage you have, how do you pay off your mortgage?

1. Use a first-payment strategy. When you get a loan to buy a house, make your first payment on the day your loan is activated. In other words, make the payment that day, before the interest kicks in, and you save months and maybe years on your loan because all that payment goes directly to the principle. Principle and interest are important to pay attention to. If your monthly payment is $1,000, only a small portion of that actually goes to your principle; the vast majority of your early payments in a thirty-year loan go to pay for interest. So you end up paying for a house three times. But if your bank will let you do a first-payment strategy, you'll save a lot.

2. Use a split-payment strategy. Instead of making one payment a month, make half payments every fourteen days. So if you owe $1,000 at the end of the month, instead, pay $500 every two weeks. That does a couple of things for you. When the year is up, you will have made twenty-six half payments, or thirteen full payments. That means you've made an extra payment that calendar year. Every extra payment cuts down on interest and will take years off your loan. I don't think God wants anybody to wait thirty years to pay off a house.

3. Make additional principal payments. As we saw a moment ago, for the first twenty or so years of a thirty-year loan, most of what you pay goes to interest. If you pay just a small additional amount each month, and indicate that you want it to go toward principal, not interest, you will also cut years off your loan. For example, let's say your monthly loan payment is $1,000. According to the amortization

schedule for next month, that means you will pay one hundred dollars toward the principal and $900 in interest. The month after that, it will be $101 toward the principal and $899 in interest. So instead of just paying $1,000, pay $1,101. Be sure to indicate that you want that extra amount to go toward principal. The next month you add on $102, or whatever the schedule tells you your principal is for the following month. If you do this consistently, you'll take months, and sometimes years, off your loan.

4. Get a loan or a refinanced loan for a shorter term. Who said a house loan has to be thirty years? That's not in the Bible. Most people don't even realize they have options. If you get a fifteen-year loan, your monthly payment may not be much more than if you had a thirty-year loan. The interest rate may even be lower because it's in the bank's best interest to get rid of it quicker. You'll save a lot of money. With a thirty-year loan on a $100,000 house, you will eventually pay about $300,000 with interest. With a fifteen-year loan on the same house, however, you might pay $200,000. You could come down even lower, based on what you're able to pay.

5. Refinance your house at a lower interest rate. As I write this, the mortgage situation is so bad that banks, for the most part, aren't giving out much credit, and even when they do, the interest rate can be high. Compare what you're currently paying with what is being offered, minus what you must pay for closing, and you may save even one percentage point, which is huge. Whenever you can cut interest, you will save money. Be sure there is no prepayment penalty on your loan.

10. Pay off your car loan as soon as you can.

There are a number of ways to do this. Let's say you've got an old car and you're ready to get rid of it and get a new car. Don't sell your old car to the dealer. Why? It's a rip-off. They will not give you what your car is worth. You can get a much greater value if you sell it yourself, or even if you use a service like CarMax, although that's not as good as it used to be. Don't sell it to the dealer because it will rip you off. Then use that cash and any other available cash for your down payment. You're going into the loan with the goal of paying it off, so you want your down payment to cover as much of the loan as you can.

If you have to get a car loan, be creative. John Avanzini recommends setting up two loans. One of them can be a ninety-day interest-only loan for the entire amount. Your goal is then to turn around and have a ninety-day pay-down marathon where you and your family do everything you can to raise as much cash as you can. You come back after those ninety days and put that extra money on the loan. Then you get a regular loan with a smaller payment and interest. Pay it off as quickly as you can, as soon as possible. Don't play with it. Once you have paid the car off, you get to the next strategy.

After you've paid off your car loan, keep making your car payments—except make them to yourself. If you were paying $250 a month for your car note, after you've paid it off, still make $250 payments, except keep that money in a savings account. That is a great investment plan. Let's say you paid off the car after two years, and you keep paying yourself for three more years, month after month. After one year, you have $3,000. After three years, you've got $9,000. Now you've got that to put toward a car. Once you sell your old car, you may have enough to buy a new one with cash. If you keep doing this, you'll be able to drive better and better cars. You may not make a lot of money, but you'll be driving around in a Mercedes-Benz that's all paid for—because you implemented this strategy. Eventually you'll be able to pay cash for your next car. That is the best way to buy a car.

Day 26

"I Am Debt-free!"

TODAY IS OUR LAST READING DAY IN THE TWENTY-EIGHT-DAY challenge to recession-proof your house. We are going to cover one final and very important thing you can do to declare war on debt.

11. Call yourself debt-free.

Romans chapter 4 tells us about how God called Abraham—and it tells us a lot about how God operates. "(As it is written, I have made thee a father of many nations,) before him whom he believed, even God, who quickeneth the dead, and calleth those things which be not as though they were" (v. 17). God said that to Abraham before he was even a father of one. He looked at Abraham, who was not the father of many nations, and called him that. He eventually got Abraham to do the same thing. Abram changed his name to Abraham and his wife's name from Sarai to Sarah. He started calling himself "the father of many nations" and his wife "the mother of many nations."

Mark 11:23 says, "If you speak to a mountain and you tell it to move, it will move" (paraphrased). Now, you may not see it move, but you walk around talking about it in faith as if it did move. "Did you see that mountain move? That's a moved mountain!" Faith doesn't wait until it sees it to say it. Faith says it until it sees it. In Mark chapter 5, the woman with the issue of blood said, "The moment I touch His clothes, I'll be healed." I bet she said it over and over again. And guess what? The moment she touched His clothes, she was healed.

Ultimately, this comes down to faith.[5] It comes down to seeing it on the inside, believing it in your heart, speaking it with your mouth, and only saying what God said about it. You need to stop saying, "I'm deep in debt," "I don't know what I'm going to do," "I can't pay the car bill," "Gas prices are too high."

What needs to come out of your mouth is, "I am debt-free. Thank God, I am debt-free!" Every morning I get up and I declare that I am debt-free. "I am out of debt. My needs are met. I have a full store to spread the Word more. I'm a God-made millionaire. In fact, I'm a God-made billionaire."

You may say, "But you're lying, Pastor. You're not a billionaire yet. You're not even a millionaire yet." Maybe I'm not in the natural, but in the spirit realm I am. And I know as I say it, as I see it on the inside and I believe it and speak it and praise God for it, it's going to come to pass. I do this because the Lord told me to do it. He said, "Call yourself a God-made millionaire."

I said, "How can I say that, Lord? Show me Scripture for that." And He did. He took me to Genesis and showed me Abraham. He told me, "I told him to call himself father of many nations before he ever was.

He wasn't even believing to be the father of many nations. He just wanted to be the father of one."

That's how I was. I thought, *I don't have to be a millionaire. I'm not one of those people who just have to have millions of dollars.*

But God said to me, "That may not be your plan for your life, but it's My plan for your life. I need you to have millions." Once I saw that He did that with Abraham, I realized I needed to start saying what God said about me. I needed to start agreeing with what He says in His Word and what He said to my heart. I needed my words to agree with His words.

Once I started doing that, He said, "It's gotten too easy for you. Now you need to start calling yourself a God-made billionaire."

So I said, "Well, so be it. I'm calling myself a God-made billionaire." As far as I'm concerned, you're reading a book written by a billionaire. I'm looking for churches that are trying to build buildings and do ministry projects, and I'm paying them off for them. That's what I'm doing. That's what I see because that's what I am—a God-made billionaire. And that starts with the fact that I'm debt-free.

Go find a single mother who is barely making it and say, "Come with me to the grocery store, and fill up your cart. Don't worry about the cost. Just get what you need. Jesus loves you." Now imagine an army of believers doing that.

You've got to see that on the inside. When it comes time to pay bills, you just sit down and say, "There's a light bill. I'll pay that. There's the water bill. I'll pay that. No car bill; it's paid for. The house is paid for. I don't have any school loans. I've got all this money sitting here that

I used to use to pay for my debt. Now I just need to go find somebody and be a blessing to him or her."

I've got plans, you understand. I'm already saying, "Hey, I know how much money I'm going to have every month just sitting there with no debt it needs to go to. It's not assigned to anybody. I'm debt-free, and I'm going to be a great blessing to people."

That's what it really comes down to—getting to a place where you can take that money and say to someone, "How much do you owe on that car? Let me just write you a check."

Go find a single mother who is barely making it and say, "You know what? You don't have any food, do you? You don't have any money for food. Come with me to the grocery store, and fill up your cart. No, no, don't worry about the cost. Don't worry. Just get what you need. In fact, get about a month's worth of food. Go ahead and just do it. Yeah, go ahead and do that. Jesus loves you."

Or you see a stranger on the corner and find out what he needs and say, "Oh, really? Let me help you out and let me tell you about Jesus in the process."

Now imagine an army of believers doing that. That's us. That's our future. People are going to be looking for believers like that because they know they've got money and they're always giving it. We're always telling them about Jesus; they may not care, but they want what we're giving them. So they're going to hear about Jesus again and again and again and again and again. Finally, they're going to hear it one more time, and they'll see the truth and get born again.

Now, isn't that incentive enough to be debt-free? Hallelujah!

One more thing about faith. Because Abraham was strong in faith, he gave glory to God before he ever became "the father of many nations." So we ought to give God praise and glory and rejoice before Him as if we're already debt-free because we believe what God says about our life, and what we say is a done deal.

So thank Him for it. "Thank You, Lord, that I'm debt-free. Thank you, Lord, that we're debt-free. Thank you, Lord, that You provided all our need, that we always have sufficiency in all things. Thank You for it, Lord. Our houses are paid off. Our cars are paid off. Our school loans are paid off. Our credit cards are paid off. Every debt is paid off for everyone reading this book. Thank You for it, Lord!"

When you get up in the morning, praise God that you're debt-free. When you go to bed at night, praise God that you're debt-free. Take one of those bills and write across it "paid for" and put it in front of you. You can keep the vision in front of you that you are debt-free. And every time you pay off a debt, have your own burn-the-note ceremony. Go ahead and burn that thing and dance and shout and rejoice because God is doing exactly what He said.

You'll get to the place that we read about in Deut. 28:1, 13. "The Lord thy God will set thee on high above all nations of the earth. . . . The Lord shall make thee the head, and not the tail." God will actually make you financially rich. Why? So you can be a blessing to the world to come. Go ahead and proclaim it: "Debt, not in my house! Prosperity, yes, you are welcome in my house!" It's time to start bragging on God. Boast about Him to the devil. Let him know you're debt-free and untouchable. Your house is recession-proof. Debt? Not in my house!

Day 27

GROUP DISCUSSION

Action point: Declare war on debt.

Action Scripture: "Then she came and told the man of God. And he said, Go, sell the oil, and pay thy debt, and live thou and thy children of the rest" (2 Kings 4:7).

Action step: Develop your debt-cancellation plan (you can be working on this throughout the week, and then discuss it when you meet as a group):

1. List all your debts with interest rates and terms.

2. Develop a monthly budget.

3. Determine what your "piece of money" will be.

4. Determine the order in which debts will be paid off.

Questions:

1. What did you read in our study this week that surprised you? That caused you to change how you thought about God and His ways? That motivated you to continue on the twenty-eight-day challenge?

2. What are some of the negative consequences of debt?

3. Are credit cards or some other debt supporting your lifestyle?

4. What things can you cut from your spending to have "a piece of money" to put toward your debt?

5. If you were debt-free, what could you do that you can't do now?

6. How do you need to change what you say about your financial situation, about whom God has called you to be, about the economic situation around you? What does God say about you that you need to start agreeing with? Where have you not agreed with it, and how can you change that?

Day 28

CELEBRATE!

TODAY, THANK GOD FOR HELPING YOU TO BE DEBT-FREE. Declare that your house is recession-proof. Proclaim, "Not in my house!"

Testimonies

THESE ARE THE TESTIMONIES OF REAL PEOPLE WHO'VE MADE the decision to follow the financial principles in this book. They've all declared, "Not in my house!"—and you can see the results.

I recently learned the importance of giving God what belongs to Him (His 10 percent), and I started giving God His tithe in full. At the time, I was doing everything I could to save, but I just wasn't able to save how I wanted to. I am a teacher, attend graduate school, and live by myself, so all the bills are mine—but God provided a way. At the beginning of the month, one of my clients made me an offer. (I help families of children with autism so I can make extra money.) The family has an apartment in its basement and offered it to me rent-free! The only thing they asked of me was to help them a few hours on the weekends, which is what I already do. Now I am in a position to save 70 percent of my entire paycheck for as long as I can. God is so good!

—V. Crafton

My husband and I were laid off from our jobs in March 2008. During that time, we went through our wilderness experience. We had no money, and every utility was cut off. Before this happened, we were tithers and sowers, so we put God in remembrance of His Word, and He sent laborers to give and meet our needs. In August, someone from the job that I had been laid off from called me back to work and gave me more money than I had originally made—and more jobs than I can contain.

— L. Harmon

In January 2008, my husband was injured while playing basketball. We were expecting our son and wondering where the money would come from to afford all the necessities for the new baby. We tithed and gave offerings the same as we did when he was working, if not more. Before the baby arrived, we received a call from our lawyer saying that we had overpaid a bill, and we received a refund. We were able to buy all the things we needed for the baby before his arrival. God is so good!

— D. Taft

Earlier this year, the company I worked for merged with another company and offered a severance package for those who would voluntarily leave the company. I prayed, and God directed me to accept this package. I'm fifty-five years old, and to the world, leaving one job to find a new one at my age may seem like a strange thing to do. But the Word says the foolishness of God is wiser than man's wisdom. God led me to stand on Hab. 2:2 and had me write the vision of the job that I desired.

In June, I left the company and started applying for jobs. For four months, I went on several interviews and was not selected. Although it was never said, I know for many of those jobs, it was because of my age. Throughout this time, God provided for me with money from the severance package.

Now He has answered my prayer and fulfilled the vision He had me write. The week of Thanksgiving, I start working at my new job. The salary and benefits are far above those of my previous job. At a time when the world is going through an economic recession and at the end of the year, when many companies are not hiring full-time employees, God is blessing my house. There's no lack of God's blessings. Not in my house!

— M. Young

I had been praying for financial increase. God began to show me areas of financial devour in my life and let me know until I corrected those areas increase would not matter. I began to cut coupons, watch late fees, we had no cable or internet and no more NSF's do to untimely bookkeeping (just to name a few). After, I began to apply these very simple financial adjustments God began to open more doors. In March of this year, God opened a door for promotion within my job, this was major because promotion had intentionally been blocked for the last 5 years, but God kept telling me to be still, be still. Suddenly, I was moved from under my boss and place directly under the Director. In an instant, God moved away the three layers of leadership that tried of break me. Praise the Lord!! God is still in the blessing business!

—M. Hamilton

SCRIPTURES ABOUT FINANCIAL PROSPERITY

T HE FOLLOWING ARE JUST SOME OF THE SCRIPTURES IN THE Bible that illustrate God's desire and capability to prosper His people financially.

"And God blessed them, and God said unto them, Be fruitful, and multiply, and replenish the earth, and subdue it: and have dominion over the fish of the sea, and over the fowl of the air, and over every living thing that moveth upon the earth" (Gen. 1:28).

"And the Lord God formed man of the dust of the ground, and breathed into his nostrils the breath of life; and man became a living soul. And the Lord God planted a garden eastward in Eden; and there he put the man whom he had formed. . . . And the gold of that land is good: there is bdellium and the onyx stone" (Gen. 2:7-8, 12).

"Now the Lord had said unto Abram, Get thee out of thy country, and from thy kindred, and from thy father's house, unto a land that I will shew thee: and I will make of thee a great nation, and I will bless thee, and make thy name great; and thou shalt be a blessing. . . . And the Lord hath blessed my master greatly; and he is become great: and he hath given him flocks, and herds, and silver, and gold, and menservants, and maidservants, and camels, and asses" (Gen. 12:1-2; 24:35).

"Then Isaac sowed in that land, and received in the same year an hundredfold: and the Lord blessed him. And the man waxed great, and went forward, and grew until he became very great: for he had possession of flocks, and possession of herds, and great store of servants: and the Philistines envied him. . . . And Abimelech said unto Isaac, Go from us; for thou art much mightier than we" (Gen. 26:12-14, 16).

"And he said unto him, Thou knowest how I have served thee, and how thy cattle was with me. For it was little which thou hadst before I came, and it is now increased unto a multitude; and the Lord hath blessed thee since my coming: and now when shall I provide for mine own house also? . . . And the man increased exceedingly, and had much cattle, and maidservants, and menservants, and camels, and asses. . . . And ye know that with all my power I have served your father" (Gen. 30:29-30, 43; 31:6).

"Thou shalt be over my house, and according unto thy word shall all my people be ruled: only in the throne will I be greater than thou. And Pharaoh said unto Joseph, See, I have set thee over all the land of Egypt. And Pharaoh took off his ring from his hand, and put it upon Joseph's hand, and arrayed him in vestures of fine linen, and put a gold chain about his neck; and he made him to ride in the second chariot which he had; and they cried before him, Bow the knee: and he made him ruler over all the land of Egypt" (Gen. 41:40-43).

"And the children of Israel did according to the word of Moses; and they borrowed of the Egyptians jewels of silver, and jewels of gold, and raiment: and the Lord gave the people favour in the sight of the Egyptians, so that they lent unto them such things as they required. And they spoiled the Egyptians" (Exod. 12:35-36).

"And it shall be, when the Lord thy God shall have brought thee into the land which he sware unto thy fathers, to Abraham, to Isaac, and to Jacob, to give thee great and goodly cities, which thou build-edst not, and houses full of all good things, which thou filledst not, and wells digged, which thou diggedst not, vineyards and olive trees, which thou plantedst not; when thou shalt have eaten and be full" (Deut. 6:10-11).

"Wherefore it shall come to pass, if ye hearken to these judgments, and keep, and do them, that the Lord thy God shall keep unto thee the covenant and the mercy which he sware unto thy fathers: and he will love thee, and bless thee, and multiply thee: he will also bless the fruit of thy womb, and the fruit of thy land, thy corn, and thy wine, and thine oil, the increase of thy kine, and the flocks of thy sheep, in the land which he sware unto thy fathers to give thee. Thou shalt be blessed above all people: there shall not be male or female barren among you, or among your cattle" (Deut. 7:12-14).

"For the Lord thy God bringeth thee into a good land, a land of brooks of water, of fountains and depths that spring out of valleys and hills; a land of wheat, and barley, and vines, and fig trees, and pome-granates; a land of oil olive, and honey; a land wherein thou shalt eat bread without scarceness, thou shalt not lack any thing in it; a land whose stones are iron, and out of whose hills thou mayest dig brass. When thou hast eaten and art full, then thou shalt bless the Lord thy God for the good land which he hath given thee" (Deut. 8:7-10).

"Beware that thou forget not the Lord thy God, in not keeping his commandments, and his judgments, and his statutes, which I command thee this day: lest when thou hast eaten and art full, and hast built goodly houses, and dwelt therein; and when thy herds and thy flocks multiply, and thy silver and thy gold is multiplied, and all that thou hast is multiplied. . . . But thou shalt remember the Lord thy God: for it is he that giveth thee power to get wealth, that he may establish his covenant which he sware unto thy fathers, as it is this day" (Deut. 8:11-13, 18).

"And it shall come to pass, if thou shalt hearken diligently unto the voice of the Lord thy God, to observe and to do all his commandments which I command thee this day, that the Lord thy God will set thee on high above all nations of the earth: and all these blessings shall come on thee, and overtake thee, if thou shalt hearken unto the voice of the Lord thy God. . . . The Lord shall command the blessing upon thee in thy storehouses, and in all that thou settest thine hand unto; and he shall bless thee in the land which the Lord thy God giveth thee. . . . And the Lord shall make thee plenteous in goods, in the fruit of thy body, and in the fruit of thy cattle, and in the fruit of thy ground, in the land which the Lord sware unto thy fathers to give thee. The Lord shall open unto thee his good treasure, the heaven to give the rain unto thy land in his season, and to bless all the work of thine hand: and thou shalt lend unto many nations, and thou shalt not borrow. And the Lord shall make thee the head, and not the tail; and thou shalt be above only, and thou shalt not be beneath; if that thou hearken unto the commandments of the Lord thy God, which I command thee this day, to observe and to do them" (Deut. 28:1-2, 8, 11-13).

"So king Solomon exceeded all the kings of the earth for riches and for wisdom. And all the earth sought to Solomon, to hear his wisdom, which God had put in his heart. And they brought every man his present, vessels of silver, and vessels of gold, and garments, and armour, and spices, horses, and mules, a rate year by year" (1 Kings 10:23-25).

"And it shall be, that thou shalt drink of the brook; and I have commanded the ravens to feed thee there. So he went and did according unto the word of the Lord: for he went and dwelt by the brook Cherith, that is before Jordan. And the ravens brought him bread and flesh in the morning, and bread and flesh in the evening; and he drank of the brook. And it came to pass after a while, that the brook dried up, because there had been no rain in the land. And the word of the Lord came unto him, saying, Arise, get thee to Zarephath, which belongeth to Zidon, and dwell there: behold, I have commanded a widow woman there to sustain thee. So he arose and went to Zarephath. And when he came to the gate of the city, behold, the widow woman was there gathering of sticks: and he called to her, and said, Fetch me, I pray thee, a little water in a vessel, that I may drink. And as she was going to fetch it, he called to her, and said, Bring me, I pray thee, a morsel of bread in thine hand. And she said, As the Lord thy God liveth, I have not a cake, but an handful of meal in a barrel, and a little oil in a cruse: and, behold, I am gathering two sticks, that I may go in and dress it for me and my son, that we may eat it, and die. And Elijah said unto her, Fear not; go and do as thou hast said: but make me thereof a little cake first, and bring it unto me, and after make for thee and for thy son. For thus saith the Lord God of Israel, The barrel of meal shall not waste, neither shall the cruse of oil fail, until the day that the Lord sendeth rain upon the earth. And she went and did according to the saying of Elijah: and she, and he, and her house, did eat many days. And the barrel of meal wasted not, neither did the cruse of oil fail, according to the word of the Lord, which he spake by Elijah" (1 Kings 17:4-16).

"Now there cried a certain woman of the wives of the sons of the prophets unto Elisha, saying, Thy servant my husband is dead; and thou knowest that thy servant did fear the Lord: and the creditor is come to take unto him my two sons to be bondmen. And Elisha said unto her, What shall I do for thee? tell me, what hast thou in the house? And she said, Thine handmaid hath not any thing in the house, save a pot of oil. Then he said, Go, borrow thee vessels abroad of all thy neighbours, even empty vessels; borrow not a few. And when thou art come in, thou shalt shut the door upon thee and upon thy sons, and shalt pour out into all those vessels, and thou shalt set aside that which is full. So she went from him, and shut the door upon her and upon her sons, who brought the vessels to her; and she poured out. And it came to pass, when the vessels were full, that she said unto her son, Bring me yet a vessel. And he said unto her, There is not a vessel more. And the oil stayed. Then she came and told the man of God. And he said, Go, sell the oil, and pay thy debt, and live thou and thy children of the rest" (2 Kings 4:1-7).

"And Elisha came again to Gilgal: and there was a dearth in the land; and the sons of the prophets were sitting before him: and he said unto his servant, Set on the great pot, and seethe pottage for the sons of the prophets. And one went out into the field to gather herbs, and found a wild vine, and gathered thereof wild gourds his lap full, and came and shred them into the pot of pottage: for they knew them not. So they poured out for the men to eat. And it came to pass, as they were eating of the pottage, that they cried out, and said, O thou man of God, there is death in the pot. And they could not eat thereof. But he said, Then bring meal. And he cast it into the pot; and he said,

Pour out for the people, that they may eat. And there was no harm in the pot" (2 Kings 4:38-41).

"And there came a man from Baalshalisha, and brought the man of God bread of the firstfruits, twenty loaves of barley, and full ears of corn in the husk thereof. And he said, Give unto the people, that they may eat. And his servitor said, What, should I set this before an hundred men? He said again, Give the people, that they may eat: for thus saith the Lord, They shall eat, and shall leave thereof. So he set it before them, and they did eat, and left thereof, according to the word of the Lord" (2 Kings 4:42-44).

"Then Elisha said, Hear ye the word of the Lord; Thus saith the Lord, To morrow about this time shall a measure of fine flour be sold for a shekel, and two measures of barley for a shekel, in the gate of Samaria. . . . And the people went out, and spoiled the tents of the Syrians. So a measure of fine flour was sold for a shekel, and two measures of barley for a shekel, according to the word of the Lord" (2 Kings 7:1, 16).

"Then spake Elisha unto the woman, whose son he had restored to life, saying, Arise, and go thou and thine household, and sojourn wheresoever thou canst sojourn: for the Lord hath called for a famine; and it shall also come upon the land seven years. And the woman arose, and did after the saying of the man of God: and she went with her household, and sojourned in the land of the Philistines seven years. And it came to pass at the seven years' end, that the woman returned out of the land of the Philistines: and she went forth to cry unto the king for her house and for her land. And the king talked with Gehazi the servant of the man of God, saying, Tell me, I pray thee, all the great things that Elisha hath done. And it came to pass, as he was telling the king how he had restored a dead body to life, that, behold, the woman, whose son he had restored to life, cried to the king for her house and for her land. And Gehazi said, My lord, O king, this is the woman, and this is her son, whom Elisha restored to life. And when the king asked the woman, she told him. So the king appointed unto her a certain officer, saying, Restore all that was hers, and all the fruits of the field since the day that she left the land, even until now" (2 Kings 8:1-6).

"And the king said unto Hazael, Take a present in thine hand, and go, meet the man of God, and enquire of the Lord by him, saying, Shall I recover of this disease? So Hazael went to meet him, and took a present with him, even of every good thing of Damascus, forty camels' burden, and came and stood before him, and said, Thy son Benhadad king of Syria hath sent me to thee, saying, Shall I recover of this disease? And Elisha said unto him, Go, say unto him, Thou mayest certainly recover: howbeit the Lord hath shewed me that he shall surely die" (2 Kings 8:8-10).

"Moreover, because I have set my affection to the house of my God, I have of mine own proper good, of gold and silver, which I have given to the house of my God, over and above all that I have prepared for the holy house. Even three thousand talents of gold, of the gold of Ophir, and seven thousand talents of refined silver, to overlay the walls of the houses withal" (1 Chron. 29:3-4).

"And when Jehoshaphat and his people came to take away the spoil of them, they found among them in abundance both riches with the dead bodies, and precious jewels, which they stripped off for themselves, more than they could carry away: and they were three days in gathering of the spoil, it was so much" (2 Chron. 20:25).

"And Amaziah said to the man of God, But what shall we do for the hundred talents which I have given to the army of Israel? And the man of God answered, The Lord is able to give thee much more than this" (2 Chron. 25:9).

"There was a man in the land of Uz, whose name was Job; and that man was perfect and upright, and one that feared God, and eschewed evil. And there were born unto him seven sons and three daughters. His substance also was seven thousand sheep, and three thousand camels, and five hundred yoke of oxen, and five hundred she asses, and a very great household; so that this man was the greatest of all the men of the east. . . . Hast not thou made an hedge about him, and about his house, and about all that he hath on every side? thou hast blessed the work of his hands, and his substance is increased in the land. . . . I will not conceal his parts, nor his power, nor his comely proportion" (Job 1:1-3, 10; 41:12).

"If thou wert pure and upright; surely now he would awake for thee, and make the habitation of thy righteousness prosperous. Though thy beginning was small, yet thy latter end should greatly increase" (Job 8:6-7).

"If thou return to the Almighty, thou shalt be built up, thou shalt put away iniquity far from thy tabernacles. Then shalt thou lay up gold as dust, and the gold of Ophir as the stones of the brooks. Yea, the Almighty shall be thy defence, and thou shalt have plenty of silver" (Job 22:23-25).

"Though he heap up silver as the dust, and prepare raiment as the clay; he may prepare it, but the just shall put it on, and the innocent shall divide the silver" (Job 27:16-17).

"He brought them forth also with silver and gold: and there was not one feeble person among their tribes. . . . And gave them the lands of the heathen: and they inherited the labour of the people" (Ps. 105:37, 44).

"Praise ye the Lord. Blessed is the man that feareth the Lord, that delighteth greatly in his commandments. . . . Wealth and riches shall be in his house" (Ps. 112:1, 3a).

"Honour the Lord with thy substance, and with the firstfruits of all thine increase: so shall thy barns be filled with plenty, and thy presses shall burst out with new wine. . . . Length of days is in her right hand; and in her left hand riches and honour. . . . The wise shall inherit glory: but shame shall be the promotion of fools" (Prov. 3:9-10, 16, 35).

"I love them that love me; and those that seek me early shall find me. Riches and honour are with me; yea, durable riches and righteousness. . . . I lead in the way of righteousness, in the midst of the paths of judgment: that I may cause those that love me to inherit substance; and I will fill their treasures" (Prov. 8:16-18, 20-21).

"The Lord will not suffer the soul of the righteous to famish: but he casteth away the substance of the wicked. He becometh poor that dealeth with a slack hand: but the hand of the diligent maketh rich" (Prov. 10:3-4).

"The blessing of the Lord, it maketh rich, and he addeth no sorrow with it" (Prov. 10:22).

"There is that scattereth, and yet increaseth; and there is that withholdeth more than is meet, but it tendeth to poverty. The liberal soul shall be made fat: and he that watereth shall be watered also himself" (Prov. 11:24-25).

"The liberal person shall be enriched, and he who waters shall himself be watered" (Prov. 11:25 AMP).

"A good man leaveth an inheritance to his children's children: and the wealth of the sinner is laid up for the just. . . . The righteous eateth to the satisfying of his soul: but the belly of the wicked shall want" (Prov. 13:22, 25).

"In the house of the righteous is much treasure: but in the revenues of the wicked is trouble" (Prov. 15:6).

"He that hath pity upon the poor lendeth unto the Lord; and that which he hath given will he pay him again" (Prov. 19:17).

"By humility and the fear of the Lord are riches, and honour, and life" (Prov. 22:4).

"He that hath a bountiful eye shall be blessed; for he giveth of his bread to the poor" (Prov. 22:9).

"He that by usury and unjust gain increaseth his substance, he shall gather it for him that will pity the poor" (Prov. 28:8).

"For God giveth to a man that is good in his sight wisdom, and knowledge, and joy: but to the sinner he giveth travail, to gather and to heap up, that he may give to him that is good before God. This also is vanity and vexation of spirit" (Eccles. 2:26).

"Behold that which I have seen: it is good and comely for one to eat and to drink, and to enjoy the good of all his labour that he taketh under the sun all the days of his life, which God giveth him: for it is his portion. Every man also to whom God hath given riches and wealth, and hath given him power to eat thereof, and to take his portion, and to rejoice in his labour; this is the gift of God" (Eccles. 5:18-19).

"If ye be willing and obedient, ye shall eat the good of the land" (Isa. 1:19).

"And it shall come to pass after the end of seventy years, that the Lord will visit Tyre, and she shall turn to her hire, and shall commit fornication with all the kingdoms of the world upon the face of the earth. And her merchandise and her hire shall be holiness to the Lord: it shall not be treasured nor laid up; for her merchandise shall be for them that dwell before the Lord, to eat sufficiently, and for durable clothing" (Isa. 23:17-18).

"And I will give thee the treasures of darkness, and hidden riches of secret places, that thou mayest know that I, the Lord, which call thee by thy name, am the God of Israel" (Isa. 45:3).

"And it shall be to me a name of joy, a praise and an honour before all the nations of the earth, which shall hear all the good that I do unto them: and they shall fear and tremble for all the goodness and for all the prosperity that I procure unto it" (Jer. 33:9).

"And the first of all the firstfruits of all things, and every oblation of all, of every sort of your oblations, shall be the priest's: ye shall also give unto the priest the first of your dough, that he may cause the blessing to rest in thine house" (Ezek. 44:30).

"Will a man rob God? Yet ye have robbed me. But ye say, Wherein have we robbed thee? In tithes and offerings. Ye are cursed with a curse: for ye have robbed me, even this whole nation. Bring ye all the tithes into the storehouse, that there may be meat in mine house, and prove me now herewith, saith the Lord of hosts, if I will not open you the windows of heaven, and pour you out a blessing, that there shall not be room enough to receive it. And I will rebuke the devourer for your sakes, and he shall not destroy the fruits of your ground; neither shall your vine cast her fruit before the time in the field, saith the Lord of hosts. And all nations shall call you blessed: for ye shall be a delightsome land, saith the Lord of hosts" (Mal. 3:8-12).

"And when they were come to Capernaum, they that received tribute money came to Peter, and said, Doth not your master pay tribute? He saith, Yes. And when he was come into the house, Jesus prevented him, saying, What thinkest thou, Simon? of whom do the kings of the earth take custom or tribute? of their own children, or of strangers? Peter saith unto him, Of strangers. Jesus saith unto him, Then are the children free. Notwithstanding, lest we should offend them, go thou to the sea, and cast an hook, and take up the fish that first cometh up; and when thou hast opened his mouth, thou shalt find a piece of money: that take, and give unto them for me and thee" (Matt. 17:24-27).

"And Jesus answered and said, Verily I say unto you, There is no man that hath left house, or brethren, or sisters, or father, or mother, or wife, or children, or lands, for my sake, and the gospel's, but he shall receive an hundredfold now in this time, houses, and brethren, and sisters, and mothers, and children, and lands, with persecutions; and in the world to come eternal life" (Mark 10:29-30).

"Now when he had left speaking, he said unto Simon, Launch out into the deep, and let down your nets for a draught. And Simon answering said unto him, Master, we have toiled all the night, and have taken nothing: nevertheless at thy word I will let down the net. And when they had this done, they inclosed a great multitude of fishes: and their net brake. And they beckoned unto their partners, which were in the other ship, that they should come and help them. And they came, and filled both the ships, so that they began to sink" (Luke 5:4-7).

"Give, and it shall be given unto you; good measure, pressed down, and shaken together, and running over, shall men give into your bosom. For with the same measure that ye mete withal it shall be measured to you again" (Luke 6:38).

"When Jesus then lifted up his eyes, and saw a great company come unto him, he saith unto Philip, Whence shall we buy bread, that these may eat? And this he said to prove him: for he himself knew what he would do. Philip answered him, Two hundred pennyworth of bread is not sufficient for them, that every one of them may take a little. One of his disciples, Andrew, Simon Peter's brother, saith unto him, There is a lad here, which hath five barley loaves, and two small fishes: but what are they among so many? And Jesus said, Make the men sit down. Now there was much grass in the place. So the men sat down, in number about five thousand. And Jesus took the loaves; and when he had given thanks, he distributed to the disciples, and the disciples to them that were set down; and likewise of the fishes as much as they would. When they were filled, he said unto his disciples, Gather up the fragments that remain, that nothing be lost. Therefore they gathered them together, and filled twelve baskets with the fragments of the five barley loaves, which remained over and above unto them that had eaten" (John 6:5-13).

"But this I say, He which soweth sparingly shall reap also sparingly; and he which soweth bountifully shall reap also bountifully.... And God is able to make all grace abound toward you; that ye, always having all sufficiency in all things, may abound to every good work.

. . . Now he that ministereth seed to the sower both minister bread for your food, and multiply your seed sown, and increase the fruits of your righteousness;) being enriched in every thing to all bountifulness, which causeth through us thanksgiving to God" (2 Cor. 9:6, 8, 10-11).

"Christ hath redeemed us from the curse of the law, being made a curse for us: for it is written, Cursed is every one that hangeth on a tree: That the blessing of Abraham might come on the Gentiles through Jesus Christ; that we might receive the promise of the Spirit through faith" (Gal. 3:13-14).

"Now ye Philippians know also, that in the beginning of the gospel, when I departed from Macedonia, no church communicated with me as concerning giving and receiving, but ye only. . . . But I have all, and abound: I am full, having received of Epaphroditus the things which were sent from you, an odour of a sweet smell, a sacrifice acceptable, wellpleasing to God. But my God shall supply all your need according to his riches in glory by Christ Jesus" (Phil. 4:15, 18-19).

"Charge them that are rich in this world, that they be not high-minded, nor trust in uncertain riches, but in the living God, who giveth us richly all things to enjoy" (1 Tim. 6:17).

"Beloved, I wish above all things that thou mayest prosper and be in health, even as thy soul prospereth" (3 John 1:2).

"And he carried me away in the spirit to a great and high mountain, and shewed me that great city, the holy Jerusalem, descending out of heaven from God, having the glory of God: and her light was like unto a stone most precious, even like a jasper stone, clear as crystal; and had a wall great and high, and had twelve gates, and at the gates twelve angels, and names written thereon, which are the names of the twelve tribes of the children of Israel: on the east three gates; on the north three gates; on the south three gates; and on the west three gates. And the wall of the city had twelve foundations, and in them the names of the twelve apostles of the Lamb. And he that talked with me had a golden reed to measure the city, and the gates thereof, and the wall thereof. And the city lieth foursquare, and the length is as large as the breadth: and he measured the city with the reed, twelve thousand furlongs. The length and the breadth and the height of it are equal. And he measured the wall thereof, an hundred and forty and four cubits, according to the measure of a man, that is, of the angel. And the building of the wall of it was of jasper: and the city was pure gold, like unto clear glass. And the foundations of the wall of the city were garnished with all manner of precious stones. The first foundation was jasper; the second, sapphire; the third, a chalcedony; the fourth, an emerald; the fifth, sardonyx; the sixth, sardius; the seventh, chrysolyte; the eighth, beryl; the ninth, a topaz; the tenth, a chrysoprasus; the eleventh, a jacinth; the twelfth, an amethyst. And the twelve gates were twelve pearls: every several gate was of one pearl: and the street of the city was pure gold, as it were transparent glass" (Rev. 21:10-21).

ENDNOTES

1 Time, posted Sunday, September 10, 2006, http://www.time.com/time/magazine/article/0,9171,1533448,00.html

2 Ibid.

3 Ibid.

4 For more information on finding your assignment from God, see my book *Getting to Your Promised Land*.

5 For more information on the role that faith plays in receiving finances from heaven and supernatural debt cancellation, see my book *God Is Making You Rich*.

Recommended Resources

Andre Butler's other books on finances:

God Is Making You Rich

Getting to Your Promised Land

Living Life to the Full

Gaining Financial Freedom

Wealth of the Sinner, Harvest of the Just

The Right Way to Give

Other recommended resources:

Kingdom Millionaire Training & Consulting,
www.kingdommillionaire.com

Rapid Debt Reduction Strategies, by John Avanzini

The Wealthy Women Club, www.catherineeagan.com

CONTACT INFORMATION

ANDRE BUTLER MINISTRIES IS DEDICATED TO HELPING equip individuals to walk in the future that God has for them. We accomplish this mission through speaking engagements, "Your Future Now" broadcasts, CDs, MP3s, books, Future Conventions, Gathering Conferences, and much more. We invite you to learn more about Andre Butler Ministries and how you can be part of this awesome and mighty move of God.

Andre Butler Ministries
3059 S. Cobb Drive
Smyrna, GA 30080
www.notinmyhousebook.com
www.andrebutler.tv

ANDRE BUTLER WEB SITE

THERE'S A WEALTH OF INFORMATION AVAILABLE THROUGH Andre Butler's Web site: devotionals, video messages, and much more. If you have a prayer request, there is also a secure prayer request submission link.